Anger
Is A Choice

Anger
Is A Choice

Tim La Haye
and
Bob Phillips

Z&I
ZONDERVAN INTERNATIONAL

A Zondervan International Edition
Marshall Pickering
3 Beggarwood Lane, Basingstoke, Hants RG23 7LP, UK

This first UK edition published in 1985
by Marshall Morgan & Scott Limited by
special arrangement with Zondervan Publishing House USA

British Library Cataloguing in Publication Data
La Haye, Tim F.
  Anger is a choice.
  1. Anger   2. Control (Psychology)
  I. Title
  152.4   BF575.A5

ISBN 0 551 01219 6

Printed and bound in Great Britain by
Anchor Brendon Limited, Tiptree, Essex

Contents

Acknowledgments

The authors are grateful to the publishers for permission to quote from the following works:

Adams, Jay E. *The Christian Counselor's Manual.* Nutley, N.J.: Presbyterian and Reformed Publishing Co., 1973.

Adams, Jay E. *How to Overcome Evil.* Grand Rapids: Baker Book House, 1977.

Augsburger, David W. *Caring Enough Not to Forgive.* Glendale, Calif.: Regal Books, 1981.

Augsburger, David W. *The Freedom of Forgiveness.* Chicago: Moody Press, 1970.

Beier, Ernst G., and Valens, Evans G. *People-Reading.* New York: Warner Books, 1975.

Burns, David D. *Feeling Good: The New Mood Therapy.* New York: William Morrow & Co., 1980.

Friedman, Meyer, and Rosenman, Ray H. *Type A Behavior and Your Heart.* New York: Fawcett Crest, 1974.

Grace, W. J., and Graham, D. T. *Relationship of Specific Attitudes and Emotions to Certain Bodily Diseases.* Psychosomatic Classics, 1972.

Hart, Archibald D. *Feeling Free.* Old Tappan, N.J.: Fleming H. Revell Company, 1979.

The Living Bible. Wheaton, Ill.: Tyndale House Publishers, 1971.

Madow, Leo. *Anger: How to Recognize and Cope With It.* New York: Charles Scribner's Sons, 1972.

Morris, Desmond, et al. *Gestures: Their Origins and Distribution.* New York: Stein & Day, 1979.

New American Standard Bible. La Habra, Calif.: The Lockman Foundation, 1972.

Nierenberg, Gerard I., and Calero, Henry H. *How to Read a Person Like a Book.* New York: Simon & Schuster, Pocket Books, 1971.

Rubin, Theodore I. *The Angry Book.* New York: Macmillan, Collier Books, 1969.

Skoglund, Elizabeth R. *To Anger, With Love.* New York: Harper & Row, 1977.

Thorpe, Louis P., et al. *The Psychology of Abnormal Behavior.* New York: The Ronald Press Company, 1961.

These abbreviations are used for Scripture quotations:

KJV: The King James Version
LB: The Living Bible
NASB: New American Standard Bible
RSV: Revised Standard Version

Introduction

Are you an angry person? . . . Then join the club! So are we. We both have struggled with anger in the past. "You mean you don't struggle with it now?" you ask.

We would like to be able to answer that by saying we no longer have to face our anger. We would like to tell you that we have found the "golden key" that eliminates hostility. And that if you will follow certain techniques, you will no longer have to deal with anger. But if we did this, we would be lying . . . or at the least, be very misleading.

No, we are human like you. That's not an excuse; that is a fact. The fact that we are human is what makes dealing with the emotion of anger so difficult. You notice, we said *dealing* with anger, not *eliminating* anger.

We believe that all our emotions have been given to us by God. It is easy for us to accept emotions such as joy, peace, tenderness, and confidence as being God-given. It is harder to believe that He has given us the emotions of fear or anger. But He has.

You may not realize it, but fear, anger, and depression are among your best friends. "You're crazy!" you reply. "You guys have been in the counseling room too long." True, we have done a lot of counseling, but we don't think we are crazy.

Let's try to explain it this way. Imagine that we went to our friends' new house for a visit. They are giving us a tour and we come to the kitchen. As we look around at the beautiful new kitchen, we notice that there is no stove. The only thing we see that might be a stove is two white porcelain rectangles on the counter—one of those new Jenn-Air stoves with the burners under the glass.

We have never seen a stove like this. We do not realize that the burners have been on, because the top of the stove looks clean and white. We walk over and place the palm of a hand on the surface of the glass and say, "What's this?" What is the first thing we feel? "Stupid," you say. Well, that is probably true, but more likely we feel the pain of a hand burning.

Now let us ask, "Is the pain we first feel a friend or an enemy?" At first it is a friend. It tells us to remove the hand from the hot burner. If, however, we leave the hand on the burner, our pain becomes our first-, second-, and third-degree enemy.

Our emotions are similar to the physical pain that we sometimes experience. The painful emotions of fear, anger, and depression are our friends . . . at first. They can become our first-, second-, and third-degree emotional enemies if we don't listen to them.

When we feel physical pain, we have a choice. We can choose to let the hand burn, or choose to remove the hand from the danger. The same is true of our emotions. We have a choice. We can choose to ignore them and experience great emotional pain, or choose to listen to them and experience health and healing.

This book is about listening to the emotion of anger. It is not a book that tells you to ignore your anger or that says your anger can be eliminated. It is a book that will, hopefully and prayerfully, help you to—

1. Understand what anger is
2. Understand where anger comes from
3. Know how to recognize anger in its many disguises
4. Learn how to make choices of what to do with your anger
5. Gain insight in how to help others learn to deal with their anger

We realize that the study of the complex emotion of anger is not an easy matter. We have attempted the difficult task of wedding simplicity with professionalism. If we have leaned in any direction it is toward simplicity. Our purpose is to help as many as it is possible with this most important emotion.

This book is designed with several thoughts in mind:

1. To help you as an individual to make choices about your anger
2. To be used as a study guide for Bible classes, home study, groups, or other small groups
3. To be a resource manual for pastors, counselors, and teachers

It is our prayer that God will use this book to help you and ourselves to face, understand, and make positive, godly choices about what to do with anger.

Tim LaHaye
Bob Phillips

1.

Anger—Everyone's Problem

"I hate you! I hate you! I hate you!" said Joan to her husband Stan.

"Why don't you just shut your mouth, woman! You make me sick!" was Stan's quick retort.

Stan and Joan had come into my office for some marital counseling. Like countless other couples, they were expressing their anger and hostility that lay deep within.

Anger and hostility are not limited to husbands and wives. I have counseled young people who wished their parents were dead; individuals who could not stand their relatives and in-laws; employees who hated their bosses; and those who were disgusted with themselves and God.

Henry Brandt, one of the nation's leading Christian psychologists, has suggested that anger is involved in 80–90 percent of all counseling. I would have to agree.

"I just can't trust them anymore," said Mike through clenched teeth. Mike had been deeply hurt by a friend who had not held a confidence. His anger was destroying any possibility of their relationship to continue.

Anger is an international plague. It is not limited to the United States. All you have to do is turn on your television set to the evening news to discover this. War in the Middle East . . . terrorist bombings in Europe . . . the invasion of troops in Africa. Wars are started by angry people—and when people grow tired of injustice, their anger ends wars.

When you think of anger, what do you usually think of? Murder, rape, aggravated assault, or a bully pushing someone around? Do you see anger simply in someone slamming doors or yelling?

A murder occurs every 23 minutes

A theft occurs every 4 seconds

THE CLOCK TICKS

A forcible rape occurs every 6 minutes

A burglary occurs every 8 seconds

One Serious Crime Every 2 Seconds

A motor vehicle is stolen every 28 seconds

A robbery occurs every 58 seconds

An aggravated assault occurs every 48 seconds

U.S. News & World Report, Oct. 12, 1981

I remember a *Reader's Digest* article several years ago explaining "the tragic deaths of four employees, and the critical wounding of another." The assassin was a "Mr. Niceguy" type, the kind of man who would make a pleasant neighbor. At forty-three years of age he seemingly "went berserk" and shot his fellow employees.

Investigation revealed that his bizarre behavior was not spontaneous. Eighteen months before the tragedy he was bypassed for promotion in favor of someone else. His wife acknowledged that "from that day on he gradually became a different man." It is not difficult to imagine the mental chain reaction he experienced. As he nursed his grudge and indulged his bitterness, mulling over the injustice of the occasion, he became so emotionally distraught that he took his .38-caliber revolver to work and shot five people. One common thread of identity united the victims: they were all in a position to have participated in the matter of his promotion by his company.

Today this man is kept behind bars, estranged from the family he loves. Four people met an untimely death, and one may be crippled for life, all because of his hostility.

From childhood, you and I have been told that anger is wrong. Don't get mad. Don't strike out and hurt others with your hostility. This is true: we shouldn't hurt others with our anger. But what about all the angry feelings we have inside? What happens to them? Where do they go?

Anger Goes Underground

Angry feelings can go underground. They often don't display themselves in active forms such as hitting, pinching, throwing things, or slamming doors. They take more subtle forms like silence, irritation, resentment, bitterness, and hatred.

I have one friend who relates that as he was growing up, he said to his brother one day, "I hate you!" Quickly his mother jumped into the squabble and said, "Martin, you can say you dislike your brother, but don't say you hate him." Martin recalls, "I hated him."

In counseling I run across many who have gone underground with their anger. So far underground that they no longer consider it anger at all. Did you know that exceeding the speed limit can be a form of anger? Anger towards authority. Or take inefficiency at work, accident proneness, chronic forgetfulness, frigidity, and impotence . . . they all can be displays of anger.

There are socially acceptable ways of displaying anger— for example, the executive dart board, the punching bag, or the homemaker who thoroughly scrubs and cleans her house. "I can really get the housework done when I'm mad!" she says.

Playing sports is also another socially acceptable form of letting out aggressions. Have you ever played football? Have you been on the line when the person across from you puts his elbow in your mouth? At that moment do you experience the emotions of love, joy, peace, and patience? During the next play do you plan to shove him gently?

Let's not leave out spectator sports such as boxing, judo, and karate. Sometimes there is a sense of pleasure that is vicarious—that is, letting someone else do the job for you.

Is Anger Always Bad?

You may ask, "Are you saying that all anger is bad? Are there not times when anger is good?"

The truth of the matter is that anger in itself is neither good nor bad. It is just anger. It is an emotion. The problem is not the experience of feeling or anger . . . at first. The problem with anger is the direction in which it leads you. Or better stated, which direction you allow your anger to go.

When anger is allowed to go in the wrong direction, we call the results bad or unhealthy. When anger is allowed to go in the right direction, we call it good or healthy. An example of good or healthy anger can be seen in the case of someone hurting a member of your family. Your anger will motivate you to leap into action to rescue him or her. It is healthy to be angry toward injustice. Anger can get you to walk again after an accident when the doctors say you will never walk again: you want to prove them wrong. Archibald Hart said, "If we could get angry only at what Jesus got angry at, we would make a wonderful world." You see, anger is a choice. You decide which way it will turn.

"But I'm not always sure what I am angry about," you say. "Sometimes people say I am angry, but I don't realize it at the time."

Before it is possible to work on any problem effectively, we first have to recognize the problem itself. In the next chapter we will take a candid look at the many different faces of anger. You will meet the Angry Family and their relatives. Any resemblance between this Angry Family and your family is purely intentional.

2.

Meet the Angry Family

Washington Irving wrote, "A tart temper never mellows with age, and a sharp tongue is the only tool that grows keener with constant use." Almost every day we meet someone with a "tart temper" or a "sharp tongue." Much of the time the tartness and sharpness is motivated by anger.

I get angry. You get angry. We all get angry. But some of us are not so aware of our anger as we should be. We will call it many things: irritation, frustration, exasperation, annoyance, moodiness, and uptightness—but never anger. I used to have a friend in high school who would pound his fist and yell, "I'm not mad! I'm not mad! I'm not mad!" Somehow I had a hard time believing him.

Now, I realize that I do not always see my anger clearly. Sometimes I get into the forest and cannot see the trees. It often helps if I can stand back and get an objective look at my anger. But this standing back and looking objectively is not easy.

I have found that as I look at the anger in others, I sometimes see myself. And I don't usually like what I see. As I see the reflection of my anger in other people's lives, it shocks me, scares me, and motivates me to change my attitudes and actions.

I would like you to meet the Angry Family and their relatives. Of course, their names are fictitious . . . and I am sure that you do not have any family members like them. But you may have some friends who do. So, it may help to look at your friend's family rather than your own.[1]

15

Andy Actor

As a child Andy used to hold his breath, scream as loud as he could, and get very red-faced. He would bite, hit, spit, and pull the hair of anyone getting in his way. As an adult he still enjoys shouting and sometimes even crying. He now likes slamming doors, pounding tables or walls, and throwing various objects. He enjoys shaking his finger in the air and expressing his anger physically through adult temper tantrums.

Tim Talker

No one misunderstands Tim. He lets all his anger "hang out" verbally. He never lets any negative issues lie. He digs them up and serves ulcers to anyone he comes in contact with.

Lucy Leaker, Paine Put-Down, and Tyrone Teaser

Lucy, Paine, and Tyrone like to serve cold cuts. They have a unique way of chopping people into little pieces. They love to make little comments like "Hi, Bill! Great to see you! Putting on a little weight, huh?" "Did you notice that pretty dress that Laura had on? It will be nice when it comes back in style." They make one wonderful comment after another and are very surprised when people are hurt. "I don't know why you feel that way. Didn't you hear me say it was a pretty dress?"

Terry Truth-Teller

Terry always tells the truth. He would never lie. "My, that's a big pimple you have on your nose this morning." Very true Terry . . . not very loving, though. "We sure had a fun time at Larry's party last night. Aren't you guys close friends? I was surprised not to see you there." Thanks Terry, I needed that. Terry's favorite comment is "I just like to tell it as it is." No anger there . . . just the plain truth . . . right, Terry?

Carmen Commentator

Carmen has a difficult time being in touch with her feelings. When Carmen's daughter fails to wash the dishes for the fourth time in a row she replies, "Marcie, I am very angry with you." Marcie, however, has a difficult time believing her. You see, Carmen speaks with a deadpan monotone voice. She has no facial expression for all her anger. Marcie is not sure if mom means business or not. If you are angry Carmen, why don't you let your face know it?

Greta Gossip

Greta has made it a practice never to say anything about someone else unless it is good. "And boy is this good!" She has been called the "knife of the party."

The Steadfast Cousins

Betty Blamer:

Betty loves to project her anger to others. It is their fault. She hasn't done anything wrong. Everyone seems to pick on Betty.

Stella Stuffer:

Stella is not in touch with her anger. She has stuffed it down inside and no longer knows what it feels like. She also sometimes has the habit of stuffing down food the way she stuffs down her feelings. Stella is a little over-weight and loves to cook. She seems to enjoy having her family and friends stuff down food also. Maybe she wants them to stuff any anger they might have.

Gabriella Gunnysacker:

Gabriella collects emotional trading stamps (hurts and disappointments) and then likes to redeem the whole book at once. She is an expert in silence. When she is collecting her stamps, she says, "I don't want to talk about it." When she redeems her emotional trading stamps, she says, "I've had it up to here!" She has a sister named **Roberta Radar**.

Polly Pouter:

Polly's tactics are the same as Gabriella's. The only difference is that you know when Polly is collecting.

Nora Nagger:

Nora has a great memory and crystal-clear critical insight. She does not forget dates, details, or events. She does not get hysterical, just historical. She has a sister by marriage called **Goldie Griper.**

The Ripumup Brothers

Clarence Creator:

Clarence is an equal-opportunity provider. Everyone has an equal opportunity to receive some of his stored-up anger. He loves a good argument. He is closely related to **Barry Battler** and **Oliver Overkill.**

Trip Hammer:

Trip is like a coiled snake ready to strike. His deadly venom of words can kill your happy emotions quickly. His other two brothers are **Steven Steamroller** and **Barlow Bulldozer.** They have a distant cousin named **Artful Revenger.**

The Ripumup Sisters

Veronica Vesuvius and Suzie St. Helen's:

Veronica and Suzie usually give you little warning as to the approaching volcanic activity. They love to "Pompeii Village" anyone with their hot lava of words. They leave you very burned up and smoking.

Sammy Saboteur

Sammy is very difficult to recognize. His anger comes in sneak attacks. Sammy is what you might call a little "passive resistive." He does not display his anger openly. He gets even by being a chronic forgetter. He loses things, breaks things, spills things, burns things, and feels very picked on and misunderstood. After all, it wasn't really his fault—it was an accident. He seems to have a lot of accidents.

Sammy is great at correcting others' mistakes and interrupting them while they are speaking. Sometimes Sammy uses boredom to cover up his hostility. He yawns, gazes off

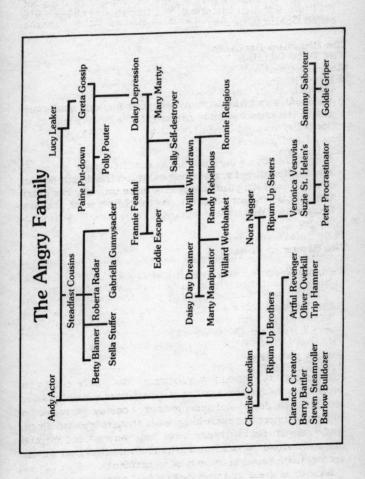

The Angry Family

Lucy Leaker

Steadfast Cousins

Andy Actor

Betty Blamer
Roberta Radar
Gabriella Gunnysacker
Stella Stuffer

Paine Put-down
Greta Gossip
Polly Pouter

Daley Depression
Mary Martyr
Sally Self-destroyer
Ronnie Religious

Frannie Fearful
Willie Withdrawn
Randy Rebellious

Eddie Escaper
Willard Wetblanket

Daisy Day Dreamer
Marty Manipulator

Nora Nagger
Ripum Up Sisters
Veronica Vesuvius
Suzie St. Helen's
Peter Procrastinator

Sammy Saboteur
Goldie Griper

Charlie Comedian

Ripum Up Brothers

Clarance Creator
Barry Battler
Steven Steamroller
Barlow Bulldozer

Artful Revenger
Oliver Overkill
Trip Hammer

into space, and acts preoccupied. One of his great tricks is to
be a sexual tease: as soon as you respond, he backs off. You
must have misunderstood him—he wasn't trying to do anything. He leaves you feeling foolish, confused, and
humiliated. Sammy has a cousin named **Peter Procrastinator.**

The Dove Cousins

Willie Withdrawn:

Willie does not like to fight. He goes for long walks and
drives. He tries to ignore his anger.

Daisy Daydreamer:

Like Willie, Daisy does not like to face her anger or anyone
else's anger directly. She escapes into her mind and there
replays her hurts and angers. In her mind she can really
tell people off. She would never do that in person; she is
too nice for that.

Sally Self-Destroyer:

Sally is Willie's sister. She wants to withdraw from her
anger so much that she withdraws to the point of suicide.
Sally has a fiancé whose name is **Daley Depression.**

Eddie Escaper:

Eddie is Willie's brother. The only difference between them
is that Eddie escapes into drugs and alcohol.

Frannie Fearful

Frannie is very afraid of what other people think. What
would they think if she became angry? She is even afraid of
her own anger. She is afraid that if she lets go with all her
anger, she would lose control. She might even lose control to
the point of losing her mind. She is afraid that God will not
forgive her for having feelings of resentment. Frannie doesn't
realize that she would worry less about what others think of
her if she knew how seldom they do. Frannie has a close
friend named **Mary Martyr.**

Charlie Comedian

Charlie is a very funny guy. He has a million anecdotes, wisecracks, and jokes. Sometimes Charlie's friends are not quite sure if he is joking or if he is really cutting them down. "Is that your face, or did your neck throw up? Just kidding," he says. "My wife, when she sits around the house . . . she sits around the house. What's the matter, can't you take a joke?" Charlie can leave you utterly defeated and gasping in disbelief. He always tries to get off the hook of his anger by saying, "You are too sensitive. I was just trying to lighten the conversation. Don't you have a sense of humor?" He has a couple of friends he pals around with named **Marty Manipulator** and **Willard Wetblanket**.

Randy Rebellious

Randy has been deeply hurt in his life. He strikes back in anger and gets even by doing things that others dislike. No one is going to tell *him* what to do. He has a superstrong coat of anger-armor.

Ronnie Religious

Ronnie really knows his Bible. He has been to Sunday school (perfect attendance), Bible school, Walk Through the Bible, Christian camp, Basic Youth Conflicts, Urbana, Young Life, Campus Life, Campus Crusade for Christ, and has a perfect church-attendance record.

Ronnie has been to Walter Martin and Ron Carlson conferences and can tell you what is wrong with every cult known to man. He can quote long passages of Scripture. He knows all about Theology, Anthropology, Soteriology, Angelology, Ecclesiology, Pneumatology, and Eschatology.

Yet, for all of Ronnie's great knowledge, he does not seem to get along well with his family, his friends, church members, or fellow workers. What do you suppose the reason is? A person with all that great knowledge *couldn't* be angry.

Ronnie is not a malicious gossip; he simply has spicy prayer requests. He does not have a temper, only intense vocal expression of righteous indignation. He really doesn't display irritability, but rather is just a bit short in speech when feeling "burdened with the care of souls." He does not hostilely reject people, just offers a suggestion that you might be happier in another church. What you might think is wrath or rage in Ronnie is just conviction or zeal . . . not anger.

In chapter 1 we saw that before it is possible to work effectively on any problem, we must first recognize the problem itself. In these pages we have taken a tongue-in-cheek look at anger in our lives. Our anger has many different faces and names. In chapter 3 we will look at an aspect of anger that is not often talked about: anger displayed in nonverbal gestures.

3.

Anger and Body Language

"Actions speak louder than words."

"Handsome is as handsome does."

"What you are speaks so loudly that I can't hear what you are saying."

Do any of these statements sound familiar? What is the thought that they are trying to convey? Basically, that our words and actions must match each other. When people's actions contradict their words what do you think most others believe? Of course, it is the actions.

To understand better why we believe actions over words, we need to look closely at communication itself. Three basic factors make up the majority of communication: words, tone of voice, and nonverbal behavior. Communication can best be illustrated by the diagram that follows:

Total Communication

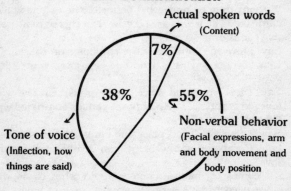

Actual spoken words
(Content)

7%

38%

55%

Non-verbal behavior
(Facial expressions, arm
and body movement and
body position

Tone of voice
(Inflection, how
things are said)

To apply the diagram, let's start with three simple words: "I love you." Now, since we are not actually sitting together, I will need you to help in this application by physically participating, if you are alone.

Speak out loud the words "I love you." Say the words several different ways, as follows:

1. Pretend you are talking to someone you know. Make a fist and hold it in front of your face. Now, clench your teeth and shake your fist toward the person in a hostile manner and say, "I love you." Do you think the person listening to your message of love will believe you?

2. Now, let's try another experiment. Do not make a fist or clench your teeth. Look at the person and say, "I love you," but this time put a question mark after the word *you*. Do you think he or she will believe your message now?

   We have removed the nonverbal part of the communication and conveyed only the actual words (7 percent) and tone of voice (38 percent). You can see that tone of voice is still the most powerful part of the communication.

Just for fun, try saying "I love you" in several other ways. By changing the inflection of your voice, you can change your message entirely.

3. Say "I love you" with no gestures or emotion at all. The person listening will not be clear about the message. Without tone or nonverbal behavior, he or she will be confused. The words are positive, but there are no positive tones or gestures.

4. Say "I love you" and place the emphasis on the word *I*. Now you are saying, "If no one else loves you, 'I' love you."

5. Say "I love you" and place the emphasis on the word *love*. Now you are saying I "love" you, as compared with "liking" you.

6. Say "I love you" and place the emphasis on the word *you*. Compared with others, "you" are the focus of my love.

When it comes to making choices about what to do with anger, we need to be aware of content, tone of voice, and nonverbal behavior. Nonverbal behavior and gestures and tone of voice give away how we really feel about things. When little Peggy stands in front of us with her arms folded across her chest, her lower lip rolled out and down and says she is not mad . . . we read an entirely different message in her actions.

The study of body language (the common name) is called "kinesics." Body-language studies help us to learn more about how we convey our angry feelings.

Body language involves a concept called "proxemics" or "territorial space." All human beings exercise what we call territorial space. Dad's favorite chair, my room, placing my coat or purse on a chair to save a seat at church or a meeting—these are all indications that we want to protect what we think is "our territory."

When territorial space is invaded, I have a tendency to become angry. If someone reads the paper over my shoulder, it bothers me. If a person of the opposite sex stands too close to my mate, I become upset. If someone fishes in my favorite fishing hole, I feel irritated. If a fellow employee crosses over into my job area and does some work, I feel threatened and uptight. If someone stares too long at me, I feel uncomfortable and then annoyed. If someone asks too many questions, I become provoked and think that it is none of their business. When territorial space is perceived as invaded, we all tend to become angry.

There are many different ways that we express our anger nonverbally. One way is through simple but strong hand movements. Although we may not say anything verbally, we still say a lot. Individuals who are angry may attempt to display their resentment through powerful sexual insults.

Sometimes an individual disagreeing with another will mock the other with the indignant thumb to the tip of the nose and the fingers waving back and forth. At certain times both hands will be used. The earliest detailed description of this gesture dates back to 1532 in the writings of François Rabelais.[1]

Other nonverbal displays of disgust, disagreement, and anger include tossing the head back, or a finger flick under the chin, or a flick of the thumb off the top teeth.

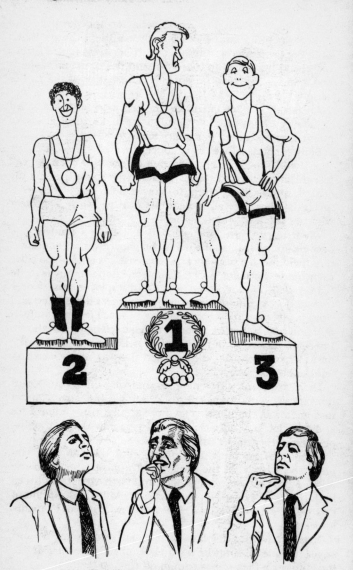

All the above gestures convey disgust, annoyance, and out-right anger. Without words they give away how a person really feels inside.

We have to be careful at this point when we read the body language of others. Just because people may cross their arms over their chest does not mean that they are closed to us or hostile. It may simply mean that this position is very comfortable to them, especially if they have a back problem. The locking of the arms may help to support the back.

We need to read body language in clusters. In other words, we should not assume from one gesture that a person is angry. Look for other nonverbal behaviors also. If a person is angry, there will be several nonverbal reactions, not just one. When people fold their arms, talk through their teeth, spit, then walk away quickly, we have a strong indication that they are angry.

The crossing of arms over the chest, the turning of the body to the side or completely around so that only the back faces the other person, the crossing of the legs—all indicate defensiveness, competition, and/or anger and hostility.

Gerard I. Nierenberg, co-author of *How to Read a Person Like a Book* and *The Art of Negotiating*, has made some interesting observations about the crossing of legs. He video-taped two thousand negotiating sessions. In these sessions he noted that when the opposers had their legs crossed,

confrontation had reached a highly competitive stage. He also comments that in the two thousand recorded sessions, no settlements were reached until everyone present had un-crossed their legs.[2]

We need to check out verbally with the other person the nonverbal signals we are receiving. "Betty, I get the impression that you are upset with me. Are you?" "John, is there something wrong?" "Laura, are you angry with me?" This checking process will help to clarify communication and will help the other person to recognize their own emotions that are leaking out through nonverbal actions. It has been my experience that many people are not in touch with their feelings. It is very difficult for some people to face the fact that they feel angry.

Not long ago an interesting experience occurred that illustrates how people do not like to own up to their angry feelings. I had the occasion to give some high school students a ride after their soccer game. I arrived before the game had ended and looked around for a parking place. I could not find one easily because there were so many cars parked together on a narrow street. I finally discovered one at the end of the street. I parked my car, began to read a book, and waited for the game to end. I was engrossed in the book when suddenly I heard a noise and became aware of a large cloud of dirt floating past my car.

I looked into the rear-view mirror in time to see a small pickup truck come sliding to a stop behind my car. As I watched, a young man got out of the truck and slammed the door. He was looking in my direction and saying something with a very angry look on his face. I got out of my car and started walking toward him. I asked, "Is there something wrong, young man?" (In my heart I knew there was.) He shouted, "The sure the *bleep* there is! All you *bleep-bleep* people parking in front of my driveway!" Evidently this was not the first time his driveway had been blocked by cars of people attending games at the school. I then looked back at my car to see where it was parked. Fortunately I was not blocking anyone's driveway.

I turned back to the young man and said, "I think I would be angry too if everyone blocked my driveway." Then he made

his classic comment, "I'm not angry. I just don't like all these *bleep* cars parked here." It was striking to hear the verbal denial in contrast to all of this young man's nonverbal behavior.

Facial expressions indicate strongly how a person feels inside. These strong feelings are picked up by those around us. A good illustration of this is found in a book entitled *Searchlight on Bible Words*. Some missionaries for the Wycliffe Bible Translators were trying to translate the Bible into the Rincon dialect of the Mexican Zapotec Indians. When they came to the sentence "I forgive you," they had a difficult time communicating the meaning to the Indians. To convey the sentence in a way that the Indians would understand, they finally translated it, "My face heals toward you."[3]

It is an interesting concept to think that our face can help in healing or it can cause great hurt and harm.

The way we stand or sit can tell others we are angry or unhappy. The facial expressions one makes indicate joy or irritation. Our tone of voice betrays our true feelings, and our body gestures signal our frustration and fury or our love and forgiveness.

As we become more aware of our own body language and that of others, we begin to see our own anger more clearly. As I become more aware of the anger I have, I am then faced with clearer choices: Do I face my anger and learn to deal with it, or do I choose to let it continue?

We have seen thus far that anger is an emotion common to us all. We have come to realize that we have a choice as to what we do with our anger. We have looked at the Angry Family and their many faces. And we have described nonverbal expressions of anger. In the next chapter we will look at how anger relates to and affects our physical health.

4.

Anger and Your Health

"I just can't do it! I've tried to stay on this stupid diet and it doesn't work! Could you give me some help?" Karen asked as she sat in my office. For the next few minutes Karen and I talked about her problem of losing weight. She told me about all her attempts with weight-reduction diets and exercise programs.

I then questioned her about how she dealt with emotional difficulties. She told me that, besides her weight problem, she did not have much difficulty with emotional problems.

"Do you have a hard time being open with people?" I asked.

"Oh, no, I can talk to just about anyone," she replied.

Acting an educated hunch, I asked, "Who are you angry at?" Surprised, she responded, "Why, no one!"

From that point it took about thirty minutes before we finally got down to some very personal issues. You see, Karen had been deeply hurt by her husband's relatives. She felt that they had been unfair to her and had been using her husband financially.

"They have never worked a day in their lives," Karen said.

"Do you hear any anger in your statements?" I asked. "Do you see any correlation between stuffing down your angry feelings and the stuffing down of food?"

Over the next few weeks, Karen gradually became aware of her feelings of resentment. Her situation does not mean to imply that all overweight people are angry, but we do know that there is a very strong tie between overeating and our emotions. We also know that one of the strongest emotions is anger—no matter how it is disguised.

He Makes Me Lose My Appetite

In his book *None of These Diseases*, S. I. McMillen cites more than fifty diseases that can be triggered by our emotions. McMillen, an M.D., wrote, "The moment I start hating a man, I become his slave. I can't enjoy my work any more because he even controls my thoughts. My resentments produce too many stress hormones in my body and I become fatigued after only a few hours of work. The work I formerly enjoyed is now drudgery. Even vacations cease to give me pleasure. It may be a luxurious car that I drive along a lake fringed with the autumnal beauty of maple, oak and birch. As far as my experience of pleasure is concerned, I might as well be driving a wagon in mud and rain.

"The man I hate hounds me wherever I go. I can't escape his tyrannical grasp on my mind. When the waiter serves me porterhouse steak with French fries, asparagus, crisp salad, and strawberry shortcake smothered with ice cream, it might as well be stale bread and water. My teeth chew the food and I swallow it, but the man I hate will not permit me to enjoy it.

"King Solomon must have had a similar experience, for he wrote: 'Better a dish of vegetables, with love, than the best beef served with hatred.'

"The man I hate may be many miles from my bedroom, but, more cruel than any slave driver, he whips my thoughts into such a frenzy that my innerspring mattress becomes a rack of torture. The lowliest of the serfs can sleep, but not I. I really must acknowledge the fact that I am a slave to every man on whom I pour the vials of my wrath."[1]

McMillen illustrates how devastating anger can be when he writes, "The famous physiologist, John Hunter, knew what anger could do to his heart: 'The first scoundrel that gets me angry will kill me.' Sometime later, at a medical meeting, a speaker made assertions that incensed Hunter. As he stood up and bitterly attacked the speaker, his anger caused such a contraction of the blood vessels in his heart that he fell dead."[2]

Do You Have a Good or Bad Stomach?

The tie between the emotions and physical well-being can be seen in all cultures of the world. Probably one of the most vivid illustrations comes from the Waffa tribe in the highlands of New Guinea. The Waffas describe their emotions through their stomach.

The Emotion	The Description
To be sorry	"The stomach is being heavy."
To be upset	"The stomach is being cross."
To be angry	"The stomach is being painful."
To lose your temper	"The stomach is being sour."
To be happy	"The stomach is good."
To think	"To hold the ear."

To convey the idea of forgiveness to the Waffas, Bible translators had to write, "Hold the ear and give a good stomach to them."[3]

In our culture we also have emotional expressions that carry with them the possibility of physical difficulties.

The Expression	Physical Ailment
"He turns my stomach."	Nervous stomach, ulcers
"He's smothering me." "She takes my breath away."	Asthma, hayfever
"I'm so angry, it shows no matter how hard I try to hide it."	Skin rashes, hives, twitches
"I was speechless with rage."	Stuttering, throat problems
"I'd like to cripple him."	Arthritis, back problems
"Hold your water."	Bladder problems
"I blew my top."	Headaches, migraines
"She was blind with rage."	Glaucoma, keratitis

I have personally been in counseling sessions when clients with anger and fear would break out in rashes, begin coughing, and have difficulty breathing. We have all heard expressions like "Don't get hyper," "Don't get your blood pressure up," or "You look as if you're going to pop."

Keep Your Wig On

Leo Madow, professor and chairman of the department of psychiatry and neurology at the Medical College of Pennsylvania, Philadelphia, explains what happens when we "blow our top." He states that "hemorrhage of the brain is usually caused by a combination of hypertension and cerebral arteriosclerosis. It is sometimes called apoplexy or stroke and may have a strong emotional component, as is shown by such expressions as 'apoplectic with rage' and 'Don't get so mad, you'll burst a blood vessel!' Anger can produce the hypertension which explodes the diseased cerebral artery, and a stroke results. Not only does repressed anger produce physical symptoms from headaches to hemorrhoids, but it can also seriously aggravate already existing physical illnesses. Even if illness is organic, anger can play an important role in how we respond to it. If we get angry at having a physical sickness and being disabled, unable to work, with added financial burdens, the anger can prolong both illness and convalescence."[4]

Norman Wright, associate professor of psychology at Biola University and a licensed marriage and family counselor, states, "Repressed anger can easily take its toll on your body by giving you a vicious headache. Your gastrointestinal system—that thirty-foot tube extending from the mouth to the rectum—reacts beautifully to repressed anger. You may experience difficulty in swallowing, nausea and vomiting, gastric ulcer, constipation, or diarrhea. The most common cause of ulcerative colitis is repressed anger. Repressed anger can affect the skin through pruritus, itching, and deurodermatitis. Respiratory disorders such as asthma are common effects, and the role of anger in coronary thrombosis is fairly well accepted."[5]

Listen . . . Your Body Is Trying to Tell You Something

There is an interesting study called the Relationship of Specific Attitudes and Emotions to Certain Bodily Diseases. W. J. Grace and D. T. Graham wrote of one hundred twenty-eight patients who were studied in a hospital outpatient department. The interviews usually lasted about one hour and took place as often as twice a week.

Most of the patients made a total of ten or more visits to the clinic. Twelve symptoms or diseases were studied. In the interviews, the first objective was to define the situations temporally associated with attacks of the patient's symptoms. After such a situation had been identified, the next step was to obtain from the patients a description of their attitude, by which is meant a clear and unambiguous statement of what they felt was happening to them and what they wanted to do about it when the symptom occurred. The results were as follows:

1. Urticaria or Hives—31 patients

Occurred when the individual saw himself as being mistreated. Felt they were [sic] receiving a blow, and there was nothing they could do about it. "I was taking a beating" and "My fiancée knocked me down and walked all over me but what could I do?" were typical statements.

2. Eczema—27 patients

Occurred when an individual felt that he was being interfered with or prevented from doing something, and could think of no way to deal with the frustration.
   "I want to make my mother understand, but I can't."
   "I take it out on myself."

3. Cold and Moist Hands—10 patients

Occurred when an individual felt that he should undertake some kind of activity, even though they might not know precisely what to do.
   "I just had to be doing something."

4. Vasomotor Rhinitis or Runny Nose—12 patients

Occurred when an individual was facing a situation which they couldn't do anything about. They wished that it would go away or that somebody else would take over the responsibility. The mucous membrane began to hypersecrete to wash out the foreign substance, to get rid of it.
   "I wanted to blot it all out. I wanted to build a wall between me and him."
   "I wanted to go to bed and pull the sheets over my head."

5. Asthma—7 patients

Occurred in association with attitudes exactly like those associated with runny nose.

"I just couldn't face it."
"I wanted them to go away."

6. Diarrhea—27 patients

Occurred when an individual wanted to be done with a situation or to have it over with or to get rid of something or somebody.

7. Constipation—17 patients

Occurred when an individual was grimly determined to carry on even though faced with a problem he could not solve.

"I have to keep on with this but I don't like it."
"I'll stick with it though nothing good will come of it."
That last two physical ailments may have given rise to the statement, "He's a pain!"

8. Nausea and Vomiting—11 patients

Occurred when an individual was thinking of something which they wished had never happened. They were preoccupied with the mistake they had made, rather than with what they should have done instead.

"I wish it never would of happened."
"I made a mistake."
Some of the individuals were feeling very guilty for an unpleasant event in their past. There has been more than one woman who has had trouble with much vomiting after becoming pregnant. Not because of any physical malfunction, but because they didn't want the baby. It is as if they were trying to vomit up the fetus. Rape victims are an example of this.

9. Duodenal Ulcer—9 patients

Occurred when an individual was seeking revenge. He wished to injure the person or thing that had injured him.

"I wanted to get back at him."
"He hurt me so I wanted to hurt him."
"She just eats me up."

10. Migraine Headache—14 patients

Occurred when an individual had been making an intense effort to carry out of definite planned program or to achieve some definite objective. The headache occurred when the effort had ceased, no matter whether the activity had been associated with success or failure.

"I had to get it done."

"I had a million things to do before lunch."

"I was trying to get all these things accomplished."

(It is estimated that there are forty-five million chronic headache sufferers in the United States. If you are a headache sufferer or the friend of one, there is hope for you—other than just aspirin. If you would like a free brochure on headache relief, send a self-addressed, stamped envelope to Family Services, 3224 W. Tenaya, P.O. Box 9363, Fresno, California 93792.)

11. Arterial Hypertension—7 patients

Occurred when an individual felt that they must be constantly prepared to meet all possible threats.

"Nobody is ever going to beat me. I'm ready for anything."

"It was up to me to take care of all the worries."

12. Low Back Pain—11 patients

Occurred when an individual wanted to carry out some action involving movement of the entire body. The activity which such patients were most commonly thinking about was walking or running away from a situation.

"I just wanted to walk out of the house."

"I wanted to run away."[6]

As you can see, there is a very complex interaction between the psychological and the physiological aspects of our being. I personally believe, along with others, that a great many of the physical difficulties we face have their roots in unresolved anger.

Blind With Rage

I recall visiting a seventy-two-year-old minister hospitalized with a severe case of glaucoma. He was basically a fine man who loved God and wanted to serve Him but, like many

Christians, he had never really dealt with his sin of anger. When I arrived at his room, I was unprepared for the angry tirade that erupted in my direction. He proceeded unceremoniously to downgrade the medical profession in general and the doctors and nurses of County Hospital in particular. After a few moments, he became livid with rage. Clasping him by the wrist, I shook him and exclaimed, "Paul, if you don't stop this, you're going to kill yourself!" Little did I realize that within two days he would die of a heart attack, although he had never experienced one before and had not been confined to the hospital for heart trouble.

Several months after the funeral, I used his case as a sermon illustration. After the service an ophthalmologist said to me, "Just this week I read in a medical journal that protracted hostility is one of the leading causes of glaucoma."

What's Smoking? . . . You or the Cigarette?

Psychiatrist and author Dwight L. Carlson relates, "Recent studies have shown that smokers have increased amounts of anger. Other studies indicate that hostility may be a precipitating factor in patients with high blood pressure. Hostility is also listed as one of the three major components of coronary-prone behavior, which tends to greatly increase one's chance of a heart attack. Patients with chronic pain syndromes also show increased levels of anger."[7]

Theodore I. Rubin, psychiatrist and author of *The Angry Book*, feels that "nearly all people have some difficulty in handling anger." He suggests that both starvation and overeating can be forms of anger. He believes that obsessions, compulsions, and phobias can have anger as their cause. In his opinion, the chronically sick and those who deprive themselves of sleep may be very angry individuals.[8]

Two counselors whom I know have noted a strong correlation between anger and individuals with pockmarks on their faces. They believe there is a strong relationship between their resentment and their skin problems.

It Was Just an Ailment

In his book *Anger: How to Recognize and Cope With It,* Leo Madow contends that accident-proneness is a form of anger.

He writes, "One outlet of repressed anger is accidents. We describe some people as 'accident-prone.' Their accidents may involve others or themselves. A man who is angry slams a door on his hand or someone else's. Or he gets into his car, drives off, and runs into someone—or backs into a telephone pole, injuring himself. A man hanging a picture for his wife when he would rather be watching his favorite sport on television will hit his finger with the hammer. His anger then expresses itself in some choice words—anger that he would not have admitted even to himself five minutes before the accident.

"An acquaintance who knew of my interest in the relationship between accidents and anger told me that he had had an accident, breaking his wrist in a fall and suffering a typical Colle's fracture, but declared that the accident was entirely unrelated to anger. 'I simply went to answer the telephone, tripped over a chair, and fell on my hand, which I had stretched out to break my fall.' I asked him for the details. 'It was a lovely day. I was working in the garden. My roses were coming in beautifully, and I was enjoying myself. I felt anything but anger. The telephone rang. My wife and daughter were inside, and I was sure they would answer it. It continued to ring and ring.'"

Madow's friend went on to explain that the unanswered phone annoyed him. In his irritation he swore to himself and then stomped into the house to answer the phone. It was in his fit of anger that he tripped over the chair. Madow's friend laughed when it dawned on him what had really happened.[9]

Accidents caused by unresolved anger and frustration are no laughing matter. Not long ago a young man had a tragic accident near our home. He was speeding through town on the freeway and failed to negotiate a turn. His car sped off the road, overturned, and was destroyed. The young man died instantly. As the police followed up the events surrounding the accident, they made this discovery: The young man and his girlfriend had words with each other ten minutes before the accident. As a result of their argument, he jumped into his car and raced away from her home . . . never to return.

Anger is a very powerful emotion. It is so powerful it can affect our health in many ways. Anger can be the cause of hiccups, frigidity and vaginismus, impotence, scleroderma, psoriasis, bruxism (the grinding of teeth together, especially at night), and some bed-wetting.

I Feel a Pain in My Chest

Heart disease is another ailment that can be triggered by anger. One of the pioneering books on heart disease is *Type A Behavior and Your Heart* by Meyer Friedman and Ray H. Rosenman. This book describes individuals prone to heart disease who are called "Type A People." The doctors describe these people this way: "It is a particular complex of personality traits, including excessive competitive drive, aggressiveness, impatience, and a harrying sense of time urgency. Individuals displaying this pattern seem to be engaged in a chronic, ceaseless, and often fruitless struggle—with themselves, with others, with circumstances, with time, sometimes with life itself. They also frequently exhibit a free-floating but well-rationalized form of hostility, and almost always a deep-seated insecurity."[10]

Later in the book the authors touch directly on aggression and hostility in the Type A person. "No man who is eager to achieve is totally lacking in aggressive spirit. Certainly we have met few if any Type A subjects who are deficient in this trait. On the contrary, most Type A subjects possess so much aggressive drive that it frequently evolves into a free-floating hostility. But excess aggression and certainly hostility are not always easily detected in Type A men, if only because they so often keep such feelings and impulses under deep cover. Indeed, very few of these men are even aware of their excess aggression, and almost none is aware of his hostility. Indeed, it is maybe only after fairly intimate acquaintance with a Type A man that his hostility becomes manifest.

"Perhaps the prime index of the presence of aggression or hostility in almost all Type A men is the tendency always to compete with or to challenge other people, whether the activity consists of a sporting contest, a game of cards, or a simple discussion. If the aggression has evolved into frank hostility, more often than not one feels, even when talking casually to such men, that there is a note of rancor in their speech. They tend to bristle at points in a conversation

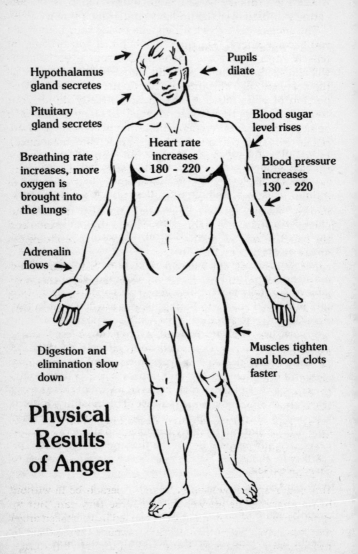

Hypothalamus
gland secretes

Pituitary
gland secretes

Breathing rate
increases, more
oxygen is
brought into
the lungs

Adrenalin
flows

Digestion and
elimination slow
down

Pupils
dilate

Blood sugar
level rises

Heart rate
increases
180 - 220

Blood pressure
increases
130 - 220

Muscles tighten
and blood clots
faster

Physical
Results
of Anger

where the ordinary person might either laugh self-deprecatingly or pass over the possibly contentious theme."[11]

The doctors explain what happens inside your body when you become angry. "On the other hand, if you become intensely angered by some phenomenon, your hypothalamus will almost instantaneously send signals to all or almost all the nerve endings of your sympathetic nervous system (that portion of your nervous system not directly under your control), causing them to secrete relatively large amounts of epinephrine and norepinephrine (otherwise known as adrenalin and nonadrenalin, or as a group, as catecholamines). In addition, this same fit of anger will probably also induce the hypothalamus to send additional messages to the pituitary gland, the master of all endocrine glands, urging it to discharge some of its own exclusively manufactured hormones (such as growth hormone) and also to send out chemical signals to the adrenal, sex, and thyroid glands and the pancreas as well, so that they in turn may secrete excess amounts of their exclusively manufactured hormones. As a consequence, not only will your tissues be bathed by an excess of catecholamines when you become angry, they may also be exposed to exceedingly large amounts of various pituitary and adrenal hormones, testosterone (or estrogen), thyroxine, and insulin."[12]

Friedman and Rosenman also say that "most Type A subjects exhibit (1) an increased blood level of cholesterol and fat, (2) a marked lag in ridding their blood of the cholesterol added to it by the food ingested, (3) a prediabetic state, and (4) an increased tendency for the clotting elements of the blood (the platelets and fibrinogen) to precipitate out. In a sense, Type A subjects too often are exposing their arteries to 'high voltage' chemicals even during the 'low voltage' periods of their daily living."[13]

Sick Questions

You may respond by saying, "Can't a person be ill without being angry?" The answer is, Of course they can. But we must realize that a lot of illness is caused by repressed anger and hostility. Also, much sickness is made more severe by hidden hatreds, grudges, fears, and an unforgiving spirit.

If you have had some physical difficulties lately you might ask yourself:

1. When did my sick feeling or sickness first occur?
2. What emotionally charged events were happening in my life at that time?
3. By being sick do I have anything to gain? Does my sickness help me to avoid someone? Does my sickness help me to avoid some task or responsibility?
4. Does my sickness help me to get even with someone? Is my sickness a weapon to make someone else feel sorry for their actions toward me? Do I gain a victory over others by making them attend to my needs? Or do I get revenge by making them adjust their schedule around me? Does it make them spend time with me that they normally would not do?
5. If my sickness is brought about by anger, why am I afraid to express it? What would be the worst possible thing that could happen if I were to express my anger?
6. If I weren't sick or feeling sick, how would I like to feel? If I weren't sick or feeling sick, what would I like to be doing? How would I like to behave?
7. What other alternatives do I have beside being sick or feeling sick? Are there ways that I could be productive? How could I help others even though I am facing problems myself?
8. With my sickness am I turning my anger toward myself or God? Am I punishing myself? Do I feel that God is punishing me? Why would God punish me? Are my thoughts that God is punishing me just because I don't understand what is happening to me? . . . Or am I afraid to face the anger I feel inside?

We can see that it is not always easy to get to the root of our anger. But with God's help and some honesty on our part, we can become our own counselors. We don't need a degree in medicine or psychology to discover the cause and correction for our behavior, although this may be helpful at times.

This brings to mind the story of the psychiatrist who went to visit one of his patients at the insane assylum. After the visit he drove out the gate and was just turning the corner when a tire went flat on his car. He stopped, took out the spare tire, and removed the lugnuts from the flat, putting them in the hubcap. While the psychiatrist was changing the tire, an inmate silently watched from the other side of the wire fence.

As the driver placed the spare tire on the car, he accidentally hit the hubcap with his foot, spilling all the lugnuts into the gutter and down the storm drain. The psychiatrist muttered to himself, "What am I going to do now?"

The inmate behind the fence said, "Why don't you take one lugnut off each of the other tires and put them on your spare tire? Then when you get to the service station you can buy some more lugnuts."

"That's fantastic!" the psychiatrist said. "That's really brilliant. What is such a smart man like you doing in the insane asylum?"

The inmate replied, "I may be crazy, but I'm not stupid!"

We may get sick at various times in our lives. The sickness may be caused by anger or made worse by anger . . . but we needn't be ignorant about it. We have some choices. In later chapters we will look closely at what they are.

The next chapter includes an Anger Inventory. It will help us to put a gauge on the anger we are experiencing at this point in our lives.

5.

Anger Inventory

What's your IQ? I'm not interested in knowing how smart you are, because your intelligence has little, if anything, to do with your capacity for happiness. What I want to know is your "Irritability Quotient." This refers to the amount of anger and annoyance you tend to absorb and harbor in your daily life. If you have a particularly high IQ, you have a great disadvantage, because you overreact to frustrations and disappointments by creating feelings of resentment that blacken your disposition and make your life a joyless hassle.

Here's how to measure your IQ. Read the list of twenty-five potentially upsetting situations described below. In the space provided after each incident, estimate the degree it would ordinarily anger or provoke you, using this simple rating scale:

> 0—I would feel very little or no annoyance.
> 1—I would feel a little irritated.
> 2—I would feel moderately upset.
> 3—I would feel quite angry.
> 4—I would feel very angry.

Mark your answer after each question as in this example:

> You are driving to pick up a friend at the airport, and you are forced to wait for a long freight train. __2__

The individual who answered this question estimated his reaction as a "two" because he would feel moderately irritated, but this would quickly pass as soon as the train was gone. As you describe how you would ordinarily react to each of the following provocations, make your best general estimate even though many potentially important details are omitted (such as what kind of day you were having, or who was involved in the situation).

Novaco Anger Scale

1. You unpack an appliance you have just bought, plug it in, and discover that it doesn't work. _____

2. You are overcharged by a repairman who has you in a bind. _____

3. You are singled out for correction when the actions of others go unnoticed. _____

4. You get your car stuck in the mud or snow. _____

5. You are talking to someone who doesn't answer you.

   _____

6. Someone pretends to be something he or she is not.

   _____

7. While you are struggling to carry four cups of coffee to your table at a cafeteria, someone bumps into you, spilling the coffee. _____

8. You have hung up your clothes, but someone knocks them to the floor and fails to pick them up. _____

9. You are hounded by a salesperson from the moment that you walk into a store. _____

10. You have made arrangements to go somewhere, but the person backs out at the last minute and leaves you all alone. _____

11. You are being joked about or teased. _____

12. Your car is stalled at a traffic light, and the guy behind you keeps blowing his horn. _____

13. You accidentally make the wrong kind of turn in a parking lot. As you get out of the car, someone yells at you, "Where did you learn to drive?" _____

14. Someone makes a mistake and blames it on you. _____

15. You are trying to concentrate, but a person near you is tapping his or her foot. _____

16. You lend someone an important book or tool, and he or she fails to return it. _____

17. You have had a busy day, and the person you live with complains that you forgot to do something you agreed to do. _____

18. You are trying to discuss something important with your mate or partner, who isn't giving you a chance to express your feelings. _____

19. You are in a discussion with someone who persists in arguing about a topic he or she knows very little about. _____

20. Someone intrudes and interrupts an argument between you and someone else. _____

21. You need to get somewhere quickly, but the car in front of you is going 25 mph in a 40 mph zone, and you can't pass. _____

22. You step on a wad of chewing gum. _____

23. You are mocked by a small group of people as you pass them. _____

24. In a hurry to get somewhere, you tear a good pair of slacks on a sharp object. _____

25. You use your last dime to make a phone call, but you are disconnected before you finish dialing, and the dime is lost. _____

Now that you have completed the Anger Inventory, you are in a position to calculate your IQ, your Irritability Quotient. Make sure that you have not skipped any items. Add up your score for each of the twenty-five incidents. The lowest possible total score on the test is zero; to attain this, you would have to put down zero on each item. This indicates that you are either a liar or a guru! The highest score is a hundred. This would mean you recorded a 4 on each of the twenty-five items, and you're constantly at or beyond the boiling point.

You can now interpret your total score according to the following scale:

0-45　The amount of anger and annoyance you generally experience is remarkably low. Only a few percent of the population will score this low on the test. You are one of the select few!

46-55　You are substantially more peaceful than the average person.

56-75　You respond to life's annoyances with an average amount of anger.

76-85　You frequently react in an angry way to life's many annoyances. You are substantially more irritable than the average person.

86-100　You are a true anger champion, and you are plagued by frequent, intense, furious reactions that do not quickly disappear. You probably harbor negative feelings long after the initial insult has passed. You may have the reputation of a firecracker or a hothead among people you know. You may experience frequent tension headaches and high blood pressure. Your anger may often get out of control and lead to impulsive hostile outbursts which at times get you into trouble. Only a few percent of the adult population react as intensely as you do.[1]

6.

The Anatomy
of Mental Problems

Our heads all jerked to attention when we heard the screech of brakes. We looked up just in time to see the driver of the noisy car throw open his door, leap out, and toss himself on the street in front of an oncoming truck. There was a second screech of brakes. The quick-thinking truck driver somehow got his truck stopped inches from the man in the street. The man in the street jumped to his feet and began to run down the alley by our office. A woman in his car slid over into the driver's seat and began to pursue the man down the alley. We ran out of the office and tried to get the license number of the car, but it sped away before we could do so. We had just witnessed an attempted suicide.

Suicide is now the tenth leading cause of death in the United States. Among college students, it is the second leading cause of death; for high school students, it rates third; and for those twenty-five to forty-five, it is fourth. The U.S. Department of Health and Human Services reports that well over twenty thousand persons die annually by their own hand. This is about one person every twenty minutes. For every person who succeeds in destroying himself, there are from five to ten times as many who make an attempt and fail. It is estimated there are more than two million people alive today who have attempted suicide at least once.

Suicide is the ultimate "cop-out" for facing the problems of life. But what about the millions of other unhappy people— the ones who do not annihilate themselves? How do they face the difficulties in their lives? Or *do* they face them? You see, suicide is one way to deal with emotions. Most individuals who attempt suicide have a great deal of anger. They are angry enough to kill . . . themselves.

Anna had been sitting motionless for hours. She did not touch her meal. She just sat and stared blankly into space. Dr. Wilson walked by and said, "Hi, Anna." Anna did not respond. In fact, she has not responded for years. Anna is in a mental hospital. She has not spoken since she entered twelve years ago.

Could Anna speak if she wanted to? She has the vocal cords. But she doesn't want to speak. She hasn't spoken since she broke up with her fiancé. What can make a person strong enough not to speak to anyone for twelve years? Anger can!

That's Depressing

Many of our emotions have an anger component to them. Consider depression. Depression usually involves anger somewhere—depression caused by other than chemical or biological changes in a person. In his book *The Psychology of Melancholy*, Mortimer Ostow writes, "Generally, even in the case of individuals who are susceptible to depression, some current insult is needed to trigger the depressive process."[1]

Ostow adds, "Depression, at every phase of its development, includes a component of anger, whether visible or invisible, whether conscious or unconscious. This anger is directed against the individual who is expected to provide love but who disappoints. At different phases, the anger may arouse a wish to irritate, to hurt, or to destroy, depending upon the degree of pain which the patient suffers. Even the rebirth fantasy carries a component of anger, for it defiantly asserts that the patient will cure himself and that he does not require the assistance of the 'parent' who disappointed him."[2]

Ostow further explains the problem as follows: "Some parents regard and treat their children with severe hostility. In these instances the child becomes fixed into a childish pattern in his relation with his parents, and subsequently as an adult is apt to have to contend with a strong depressive tendency. Overt hostility of parent to child seems inhuman and perverse, and yet we know of numbers of such instances. . . .

But even currently we read of what is now called the 'battered-child' syndrome. Small children are sometimes brought to the hospital or to the morgue showing signs of severe physical abuse. Investigation discloses that they have been abandoned or actually hurt by their parents. From time to time we read in the newspapers of a child murdered by a parent. . . .

"If we study psychoanalytically patients who harbor hostility toward their children, we find that in each case the parent, as a child, had to contend with intense anger against his own parent or one of his own siblings; that he had contrived some defensive maneuver to contain that anger, such as reactive affection, loyalty, or subservience to the hated person; and that with the advent of the infant of the new generation the defense had collapsed and the individual was left once more to deal with this overwhelming anger. . . .

"Hostility and rejection by the parent constitute a serious threat to the child. Feeling threatened, he clings more tightly, and this clinging includes both affectionate and hostile components. The intensity of these mixed feelings makes the situation traumatic. Traumatic situations tend in general to repeat themselves. The child may respond to any subsequent rejection with aggressive clinging. The child, when he becomes an adult, may attach himself to an unreliable, hostile partner. As an adult, he may provoke rejection by his partner. Or as a parent he may repeat the same pattern with his own child, rejecting the child and abusing it as he was rejected and abused."[3]

How do people get to the place where they want to commit suicide or retreat from society? It is a process. It does not happen overnight. Suicide or the choice of mental illness is a method of coping with life and its frustrations.

The Emotional Process

I believe the process first starts with a relationship of great love or affection. This relationship could be child to parent, parent to child, friend to friend, boyfriend and girlfriend, or husband and wife. Intertwined in the relationship of great love or affection are needs, expectations, demands, perceptions, assumptions, and attitudes.

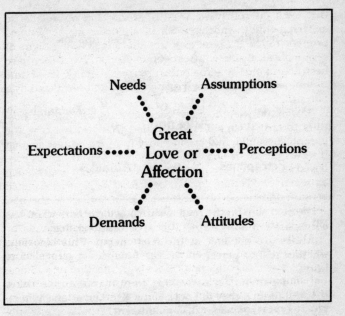

These needs, expectations, demands, perceptions, assumptions, and attitudes may be conscious or unconscious to the individual. They may be expressed or unexpressed. The expressed and conscious forms are much easier to deal with than the unexpressed or unconscious ones.

In premarital counseling I usually ask the spouses individually. "What are your expectations for your partner?" They usually have no problem in telling me what they are looking for. I then follow up with the next question, "What expectations do they have for you?" At this point they stumble. We have many expectations for others that they are not even aware of.

I counsel many couples who, having been married for more than twenty years, use the "crystal ball technique." They assume that their partners should know automatically what their needs are. "I'm not going to tell George; he should know by now." Maybe he should . . . but does he? How will he really know until the needs are expressed?

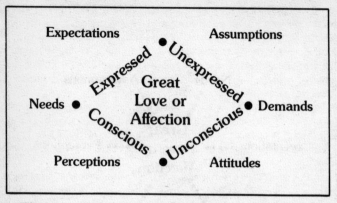

The next step on the road toward suicide occurs when the needs, assumptions, expectations, perceptions, demands, or attitudes are not met in the relationship. This blockage, whether real or perceived as real, produces a great deal of hurt.

If your parents say something to hurt you, or you think they did (even if they did not), you will feel emotionally hurt. This hurt brings about disappointment.

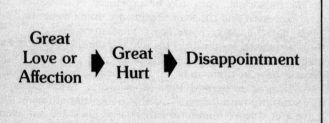

After disappointment comes anger, revenge, or fear . . . or a combination of these. The anger can be directed toward the object that caused the hurt or it can be turned inward.

If you are dating someone and you discover that he or she has been seeing another person, you will feel hurt and disappointment. You may choose to confront your partner directly: "Listen, I don't appreciate what you are doing!" Or you may choose to hold your hurt and anger inside. You think about it. You dwell upon it. It eats you up inside. You may choose revenge. Your revenge may be active: "I'll show them! I'll start dating someone else just as he (she) is." Or you may choose more passive forms of revenge: Silence, procrastination, forgetfulness, or sabotage.

You may experience fear, and you may choose to express this fear: "I am afraid to lose you." Or you may choose to deny the fear: "It doesn't bother me! It's a free country! They can date whoever they want." But inside you are dying a slow death.

If the conflict is not dealt with at this point, it creates varying degrees of frustration. The frustration then builds until we choose to do something about it. Our choice may vary according to each situation. We will most likely choose one of three possible courses of action:

WITHDRAWAL — ATTACK — COMPROMISE

The following diagram will help to visualize the various methods we may choose in dealing with our frustration or conflict. Some of the choices will be more socially accepted, and some will be less socially accepted.

Compensation

It is a form of behavior an individual adopts to offset or overcome a weakness or limitation by drawing attention to a strong or favorable characteristic or attribute. Over-compensation refers to a pattern of behavior in which the individual exerts an excessive amount of effort and energy in the function in which he is (or feels) deficient, thereby attaching overwhelming importance to this function. Transferred compensation refers to behavior in which the person directs his effort and energy toward a function other than that in which he is or feels deficient.

Rationalization

Refers to the justification of conduct, beliefs, and sentiments by giving reasons other than those which actually motivated the individual. Justification refers to giving seemingly plausible reasons to justify one's conduct.

"Sour grapes" refers to excuses given to persuade oneself and others that something which is wanted intensely but unattainable is not worth trying for. Negative sour grapes or sweet lemon (Pollyanna) attitude refers to excuses and reasons given to proclaim the desirability of an unsatisfactory condition or situation.

Substitution

Substitution means evading possible failure, or lessening the effects of actual failure, in overcoming an obstacle by selecting a different goal, usually an easier one.

Sublimation is the substitution of a socially desirable activity for the goal that is really desired; for example, the girl who fails to attract or hold a desirable life mate may become a nurse or a teacher. Perversions are where the individual substitutes asocial for socially accepted actions. However, from the individual's point of view, such behavior may serve to gain attention and to provide a feeling of self-importance.

Identification

Attaching oneself to other individuals or to groups who have become successful in attaining goals which one has found it difficult or impossible to achieve is referred to as identification.

Projection

Means imagining or perceiving and calling attention to undesirable behavior, traits, or motives in others in order to deflect attention from one's own failures, deficiencies, or shortcomings.

Egocentrism

The egocentric person attempts to gain recognition not obtained through socially approved achievement by drawing attention to himself in some other way. In college students this mechanism may take the form of telling silly and pointless jokes, eating broken phonograph records, or swallowing live goldfish.

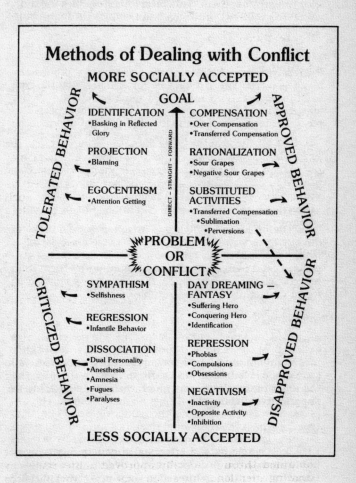

Methods of Dealing with Conflict

MORE SOCIALLY ACCEPTED

GOAL

TOLERATED BEHAVIOR

APPROVED BEHAVIOR

DIRECT – STRAIGHT – FORWARD

IDENTIFICATION
• Basking in Reflected Glory

COMPENSATION
• Over Compensation
• Transferred Compensation

PROJECTION
• Blaming

RATIONALIZATION
• Sour Grapes
• Negative Sour Grapes

EGOCENTRISM
• Attention Getting

SUBSTITUTED ACTIVITIES
• Transferred Compensation
• Sublimation
• Perversions

PROBLEM OR CONFLICT

CRITICIZED BEHAVIOR

DISAPPROVED BEHAVIOR

SYMPATHISM
• Selfishness

DAY DREAMING – FANTASY
• Suffering Hero
• Conquering Hero
• Identification

REGRESSION
• Infantile Behavior

DISSOCIATION
• Dual Personality
• Anesthesia
• Amnesia
• Fugues
• Paralyses

REPRESSION
• Phobias
• Compulsions
• Obsessions

NEGATIVISM
• Inactivity
• Opposite Activity
• Inhibition

LESS SOCIALLY ACCEPTED

Sympathism

Sympathism connotes avoiding a problem by obtaining the sympathy of others. This mechanism enables the individual to evade his problems and troubles through being "babied."

Regression

Regressive behavior refers to the avoiding of a problem or obstacle by retreating to an inferior or more infantile type of adjustment. The individual usually retreats to the status of a sick or younger person who is not expected to meet the demands of such situations as that in which he now finds himself. Being unable to cope with the problems which confront him, he avoids facing them by retreating to an infantile level of behavior and by indulging in childish forms of action such as crying, sulking, pretending illness, or temper tantrums.

Dissociation

Dissociation means refusing to attack or solve a problem directly by ignoring, evading, or otherwise dissociating it from consciousness. The individual avoids facing unpleasant and painful situations by eliminating them from his conscious experience. In this way he is enabled to forget dangerous and disagreeable episodes.

Daydreaming

Escaping from problems by solving them in imagination is called fantasy. The individual retreats from reality into a dream world in which imaginary successes are easily achieved. The pleasant dream is usually the "conquering-hero" type, in which the individual achieves superiority by doing the things he most desires. The unpleasant dream is usually of the "suffering-hero" or martyr type, in which the individual imagines himself being persecuted, mistreated, or discriminated against by persons who do not understand him, and therefore deserving of pity or sympathy. A daydreamer may gain great satisfaction from picturing himself as a martyr to a misunderstanding world.

This mechanism, if used to extremes, is indicative of severe maladjustment. As a result of excessive daydreaming the individual may fail to distinguish fact from fancy, the real from the unreal, and the practical from the impractical. By retiring from reality to a dream world, he replaces all environmental stimuli with imaginary stimuli. This process may result in the disorganization of the individual's personality.

Repression

Repression is the process of ignoring the memory of painful experiences or thrusting aside present desires in order to avoid the conflict involved in a direct solution of a problem. The individual, by denying certain tendencies or impulses, comes to believe that he does not have them. By banishing socially disapproved wishes or desires he wards off the threat of guilt feelings and thus maintains his sense of personal worth and social acceptability. Repressed emotions may also be expressed in the form of physical symptoms such as aches, functional paralyses, tremors, and functional blindness. These symptoms often provide a welcome respite from the intolerable situations which may be confronting the individual.

Negativism

The negativistic individual attempts to deny the existence of a problem or obstacle and resorts to such reactions as stubbornness and rebellion against authority. This mechanism is a device by means of which the individual avoids many disagreeable efforts required for making socially desirable adjustments; it serves as a protection against feelings of cowardice and inadequacy. In many instances the negativistic individual not only refuses to do anything about his problem, but does the opposite of what his associates think should be done.

Other Mechanisms:

Reaction Formation

A mechanism by means of which the individual does the opposite of what he really wants to do. For example, a person who desires an alcoholic drink but feels that drinking is disgraceful may walk three or four blocks out of his way to avoid passing a bar or liquor store.

Perfectionism

The individual attempts to escape blame or criticism by doing everything perfectly. This mechanism also permits such a person to feel justified in pointing out the imperfections in others.

Restitution

A mechanism through which the individual engages in some socially approved activity to make up for a socially disapproved mechanism displayed previously. For example, the mother who screams at her child "I'll kill you if you don't behave!" will buy him an expensive toy the next time she goes shopping.

Flight Into Reality

A mechanism by which the person buries himself in his work so that he will not be disturbed by the pressure of other problems. For example, the husband who is having marital problems at home goes to the office early and works late so that there will be no time or opportunity to quarrel with his wife. Similarly, an unmarried woman in her thirties may immerse herself in charitable activities so that she will have no spare time to experience the disappointments that come from having no dates.[4]

The above methods of dealing with conflict will in many cases cause the individual to experience depression and/or anxiety. This often leads the individual to lose trust in others. As trust is lost, disrespect of the person who did the hurting grows into resentment. The resentment then blossoms into bitterness and/or hatred. If the process is repeated over and over enough times in an individual's life, he or she then develops a lifestyle of dealing with conflict.

Lifestyles

Sylvia was hurt a lot as a small child. She had no one to share her hurt with, so she simply kept everything inside. She would ignore, avoid, and withdraw from those who hurt her. In fact, she began to withdraw from any situation that had an element of conflict attached to it. This withdrawal grew until she could not stand conflict in any form. When others

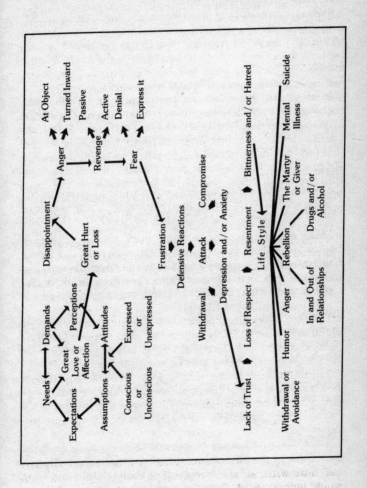

were quarreling among themselves, she began to withdraw, even if the problem didn't involve her.

Sylvia has reached the point where she doesn't see conflict. Or at least, she will not admit conflict exists. "Everything is all right." "We're all friends." Sylvia has developed a well-organized routine for burying her head in the sand. Sylvia's method for dealing with her various hurts, disappointments, and angers is to **Withdraw or avoid** them.

Bruce doesn't seem to have a problem in the world. He is happy-go-lucky. A laugh a minute. He has an endless stream of jokes, anecdotes, wise cracks, and stories. He is the world's greatest practical joker. To him, life is funny. At first it is fun to be around Bruce. But slowly we begin to wonder, "Does he ever have a down day? Doesn't he ever take anything seriously? Why doesn't he have problems like other people?" Pretty soon we get tired of his practical jokes. They are not very "practical" after a while. In fact, we may even sense a little hostility or revenge in them.

Bruce doesn't have the problems other people do, because he can't face problems as other people do. Bruce, like Sylvia, has been hurt. He learned early in life to cover his hurt and disappointment with **Humor**. Humor is a great mask for true feelings. Bruce may tell a lot of puns, but deep down inside, he is really punishing himself.

Lowell is a very angry person. He is angry with his wife, his children, his boss, fellow employees, sales clerks, and all the "stupid drivers" on the road. Why is Lowell so angry? Why does he "dump" on everyone he comes in contact with?

Lowell has been hurt greatly at some time. He did not know how to deal with his disappointment other than just to get **Angry**. Since he never resolved his anger, it grew. New situations added new angers until Lowell is now a walking time bomb.

Leann has had many boyfriends. Several have even proposed marriage. She has been engaged three times. But she just can't seem to find the right guy; each relationship seems to be more stormy than the one before. Why can't Leann settle down? Why does she go from one crisis to another in her relationships?

Leann has been hurt in her relationships. She has been

very disappointed. Her hurt is so great that she has determined not to be hurt again. She has designed a program to escape hurt, although she may not be consciously aware of it. Her plan is to **Move in and out of relationships.**

She begins a relationship and progresses to the point where she could be hurt again, as she was in the past. Then she sabotages the relationship. She does something, or does not do something, to provoke discord. When her partner responds to the discord, she says, "It is just as I thought. He really doesn't care." Then the relationship begins to degenerate and fall apart, which confirms to her his lack of caring. The cycle keeps repeating itself.

Leann may eventually get married, but even in marriage she may still keep up the "sabotage cycle." Jay Haley, a nationally known family therapist, illustrates this point: "When one spouse continues the marriage even though treated badly by the other, a compulsory type of relationship occurs. If a husband puts up with more than is reasonable from his wife, the wife may begin to assume that he must be staying with her because he has to, not because he wants to, and the marriage is in difficulty. Sometimes a spouse will appear to test whether he or she is really wanted by driving the other to the point of separation. It is as if they say, 'If my mate will put up with anything from me, I am really wanted.'

"However, if the spouse passes the test and puts up with impossible behavior, the tester is not reassured about being wanted but becomes convinced the spouse is doing so because of an inability to leave. Once this pattern has begun, it tends to be self-perpetuating. A wife who believes that her husband stays with her because of his own inner desperation rather than because he wants her will dismiss his affectionate approaches as mere bribes to stay with her rather than indications of real affection. When she dismisses her husband's affection, he tries even harder to please her and so increases her belief that he stays with her out of desperation rather than choice. When the husband can no longer tolerate the situation, he may make a move to leave her. The moment he indicates he can do without her, the wife begins to feel she may be a voluntary choice and be attracted to him again. However, such a wife will then test her husband again by extreme behavior. When he responds permissively she again feels he is unable to leave her, and the cycle continues."[5]

Bob has always been hard to live with. He has never gotten along well with his parents, his teachers, his bosses, policemen, or anyone in authority. He has been called rebellious. No one can seem to get through to him; he seems to close everyone out. What caused all this reactiveness?

Like the others mentioned, Bob has been deeply hurt. Whether the hurt was real or imagined doesn't matter: to Bob it was real. Bob's method of dealing with hurt was to choose **Rebellion.** Bob struck back at those who hurt him. When he did, they responded negatively. Their negative responses to his anger proved to him that they didn't care . . . so he struck back again. They responded negatively again. On and on the story goes. Rebellion is now Bob's lifestyle.

Craig, like Bob, also strikes back. Craig, however, chooses a different method. He has chosen **Drugs and alcohol.** His method of handling hurt, disappointment, and anger is to get "high" on pills and booze. When he is high, he doesn't have to face his emotions. It is the great escape.

But Craig really doesn't escape. He merely exchanges one problem for another. In seeking emotional release he comes into bondage to a monster that makes things worse than they were before.

Martha's lifestyle is quite different from all the others. She has chosen the lifestyle of the **Martyr or giver.** Martha has been hurt too, but she is different, because she thinks she deserves the hurt. She derives some sense of satisfaction from all the hurt. Maybe it is self-pity or attention. Whatever it is, she thrives on it and, in fact, almost encourages it.

Martha gives and gives, but she can't receive very well. Her giving helps to obligate others to her. There is a lot of control in keeping others obligated. She really can't change her lifestyle, because she might lose all that control over people. Besides, if she got well, she might have to face how hurt and angry she is.

Ken has chosen—as many have—a peculiar but predictable method of dealing with his hurts, disappointments, fears, and anger. Ken has chosen **Mental illness.**

He has tried them all. He tried the persistent, morbid

dread and fear called phobias. He then moved on to develop compulsions, those irresistible impulses to perform acts contrary to his better judgment. These led him to become obsessed with ideas or the series of ideas that would constantly torment him. He didn't want to step on "any crack or he would break his mother's back." He had to wash his hands fifty times a day and say certain words over and over.

He began to think that everyone was talking about him— and that the FBI and CIA were after him. He developed a paralysis in his legs and could not walk. He lost his memory. He became silent and then very still. He does not move. He has finally made an escape into the land of living death.

Dear Clara has not been happy for quite some time. She has been locked into a deep depression for weeks. She doesn't sleep well, eat well, or feel well. She is not well!

She is hurt and angry. She feels very unloved, unwanted, and uncared for. She doesn't feel like doing anything; she just stares and stares. Her thoughts are not pleasant. Her tears have dried up. She doesn't care any more.

Clara feels she can make but one decision. Slowly she walks to the bathroom, gets a glass of water, and comes back to the bed. She empties the bottle of pills on her nightstand. She opens her Bible to read, and she dies. Clara has chosen **Suicide.**

These examples show that we human beings are all very complex when it comes to our emotions. Each separate emotion is chained to other emotions, making it difficult to understand what motivates our behavior and the behavior of others.

In the next chapter we look more closely at the emotion of anger. We will see where it originates and how we can begin to understand and deal with it.

7.

Why Do I Get Angry?

"I'm sick and tired of those dumb kids leaving their bikes in the driveway!" Marty said as he slammed on the brakes. He jumped out of the car and threw the bikes onto the lawn. Then he angrily drove into the driveway.

He was still muttering as he reached the front door. He started to put his key in the lock when the package he was carrying slipped out from under his arm. He could not catch it, because his briefcase was in his other hand. He swore. He picked up the package and tried again to put his key into the lock. Just then his wife Ellen opened the door.

"Hello, honey!" Ellen said with a smile.

"Why don't you tell those kids to keep their *bleep, bleep* bikes out of the driveway?" was Marty's quick retort as he brushed her aside and entered the house. It wasn't long before the whole household knew that daddy was home.

You may be thinking, "Boy, is he an angry man! He has no right to do that to his family. He sure is selfish." I agree. He *is* angry and selfish. He shouldn't do that to his family. But I think there may be more here than meets the eye.

I have found that it is very easy to make quick judgments about people. It is easy to condemn, to accuse, to come up with pat answers. It is also easy to give formulas, techniques, and timely quotes for dealing with our emotions—especially anger. It is far more difficult to put formulas into practice.

In this book I will be suggesting methods and techniques for dealing with anger. Some will apply to your situation and some will not. There is no single, easy solution to the problem of anger. It is a complex emotion and usually involves a combination of other emotions such as fear, hurt, envy, jealousy, revenge, or depression.

I do not excuse Marty's actions or say they are justified. They are not. Marty is responsible for his behavior. But if we merely talk to Marty about the bikes in the driveway, we might not get through to him.

Who Is Responsible?

I said earlier that all our emotions are God-given, even anger. To this you may respond, "If all our emotions are God-given, then God is responsible for my anger." The answer is yes and no. Yes, He did give you the emotional capacity for anger. No, He is not responsible for your angry outbursts. You have a choice of what to do with your anger.

In their book *People-Reading*, Ernst G. Beier and Evans G. Valens make an interesting observation about the relationship of responsiblity and our emotions. They say that "most people like to believe that feelings originate outside themselves. Something 'happens' to them that 'makes' them sad or happy or angry or lustful. These feelings in turn cause them to behave in unusual ways.

"The assumption is convenient because it lets them off the hook. Behavior that otherwise would be unacceptable or suspect becomes 'understandable' when an emotional state is seen as the cause. If they feel depressed enough they can probably quit early, and if they are hopelessly in love they can get away with all kinds of weird performances.

"When someone is driven to take his hostile feelings out on us, we suffer and we feel helpless. If we complain, we are told, 'But I can't help it. That's how I feel about it.' The speaker is giving us a double message: he wants us to know he doesn't like us, but he doesn't want us to hold him personally responsible. He cons us into sympathizing with his apparent, conscious dilemma. What can we do if the other guy is driven by feelings he can't control?

"The answer is that we can do a great deal. The first step is to gather new information from the immediate situation. As listeners, we have much to learn from emotional displays, but we miss most of it if we get entangled in the speaker's own theories about his own feelings.

"What we need is a fresh point of view. We need to turn his cause-and-effect relationship upside down: instead of supposing that he does what he does because of his feelings, let us imagine that he has the feelings he has because of what they allow him to do. This changes our perspective and affects our hearing. Rather than searching for outside reasons to explain his actions, we listen for the inner origin of his feelings and for what he says and does in the name of these feelings.

"Take a man who yells, 'You make me so mad I could strangle you!' His anger gives him reason to do violence, to satisfy an aggressive urge he would never feel justified in following without the presence of the anger. And his anger is clearly the fault of the other person. He never says, 'I make me so mad I could strangle you.' If we listen for ways in which he might be profiting from the emotion, or even creating it, we may learn something. When the man says, 'The more I think about it, the madder I get,' it becomes pretty obvious who is generating the anger.

"Nobody can be run by his feelings unless, at some level of his being, he wants to be run by his feelings. Or, to put it the other way around, anybody who wants to do something he normally finds unacceptable can generate an emotion that will, at least in his own eyes, 'explain' and thus excuse the act."[1]

If I gave you some money, I would be responsible for the gift. I would not be responsible for how you spent the money. You could spend it for good purposes or for bad. God has given us our emotions. We can use them either to help ourselves and others or to hurt ourselves or others.

"If what you say is true, then why don't I use my emotions for good? Why do I have such a difficult time with anger?" We all have a difficult time for a number of reasons.

It has been my experience that when a person's actions or comments are out of proportion for a particular event, something else is going on.

Let's take Marty's situation. We see the events of the bikes being in the way, the package dropping, and his anger erupting. This anger is out of proportion with what is happening at that moment. Something else must be going on.

What we don't see is that Marty just missed being struck by a car at the intersection five blocks from home. We don't see that his fellow employee Bill Johnson crossed over into his territory and got some of his important clients. We don't see that his boss told him that if his work doesn't improve, he is going to lose his job. We don't see that Marty is deeply in debt because of his daughter's illness. We don't see that he holds two jobs to try to make ends meet. And we don't see that Marty is scared to death that he is not going to make it financially and feels like a failure. We really don't see a lot about people, do we?

The primary reason we have such a hard time with anger is that we have an old sin nature inherited from our great-grandfather Adam. Because his sin has been imparted to us, the healthy display of the emotion of anger has become clouded and warped.

The way we deal with anger is further complicated by our basic temperament and body chemistry. We will look at basic temperament in chapter 9.

Other influences that affect the way we deal with anger include our desires, demands, and expectations. The family models we had as we grew up affect our dealing with anger. If dad yelled when he was angry, we may yell when angry. If mom grew silent when angry, then we may copy her method of handling anger.

We are influenced not only by our families, but by the way relatives, friends, co-workers, authority figures, and strangers deal with their anger. After many personal experiences with anger we develop our own style of displaying or hiding anger.

Then, in addition to all these influences, there are uncontrolled outside forces that affect our responses to anger. If your child dies, if your house burns down, if you lose a contact lens, if someone runs into your car—all these events stimulate our response to anger.

Why Do People Swear?

As we can see, the emotion of anger is complex. Many factors influence us. Sometimes we have a difficult time expressing all the emotions that stir inside us. I personally think this

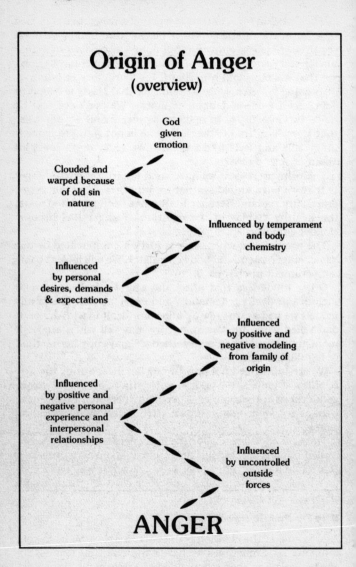

Origin of Anger
(overview)

God
given
emotion

Clouded and
warped because
of old sin
nature

Influenced by temperament
and body
chemistry

Influenced
by personal
desires, demands
& expectations

Influenced
by positive and
negative modeling
from family of
origin

Influenced
by positive and
negative personal
experience and
interpersonal
relationships

Influenced
by uncontrolled
outside
forces

ANGER

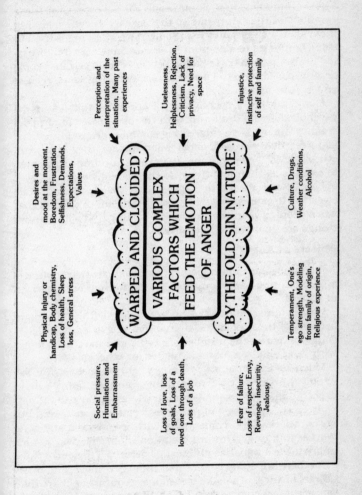

Perception and interpretation of the situation, Many past experiences

Uselessness, Helplessness, Rejection, Criticism, Lack of privacy, Need for space

Injustice, Instinctive protection of self and family

Desires and mood at the moment, Boredom, Frustration, Selfishness, Demands, Expectations, Values

Culture, Drugs, Weather conditions, Alcohol

WARPED AND CLOUDED

VARIOUS COMPLEX FACTORS WHICH FEED THE EMOTION OF ANGER

BY THE OLD SIN NATURE

Physical injury or handicap, Body chemistry, Loss of health, Sleep loss, General stress

Temperament, One's ego strength, Modeling from family of origin, Religious experience

Social pressure, Humiliation and Embarrassment

Loss of love, loss of goals, Loss of a loved one through death, Loss of a job

Fear of failure, Loss of respect, Envy, Revenge, Insecurity, Jealousy is why swearing is so popular. Many times a swear word has a host of emotions in it. Some people cannot express all these emotions at the same time so they swear, thereby releasing them all in a single outburst. Sometimes swearing is used to bring emphasis to a point or to elevate one's stature. Swearing is also used to try to gain acceptance from certain people or groups. However, I think most swearing is to release anger, fear, and frustration.

Along this line, I recently saw a TV program that featured a psychologist who dealt only with the psychology of airplane crashes. He made an interesting comment. He said that the last recorded words of most pilots before they crash are swear words. The pilots couldn't express or didn't have time to express all their emotions, so they would swear.

This is not meant to suggest that people should start swearing to express how they feel. It is meant to suggest that when people swear, they may be indicating that a lot of other things are going on in their lives.

Objects of Anger

Not only are there many factors that stimulate the emotion of anger, but there are many objects that we vent our anger on or toward.

I have counseled people who were angry with God—angry because of their looks, or angry because a loved one died. I could not count the number of people who have been angry with their children, parents, mates, or other relatives.

Much of the time we are angry with ourselves. We say wrong things, we do wrong things, and we fail. We have expectations and demands for ourselves that we cannot possibly meet. When we fail in our expectations, we take it out on ourselves. We become angry with friends and stangers. We become angry toward inanimate objects. We become angry toward injustice and real or perceived danger.

So there are many factors that influence anger, and many objects of anger. To make it even more confusing, more than one of these factors may hit us at the same time. We may also direct our anger toward more than one object at the same time.

In the next chapter we will look at the starting point for

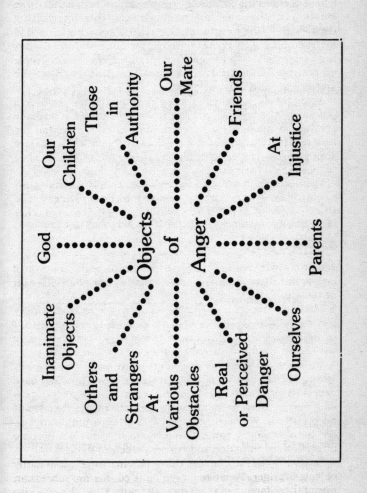

dealing effectively with anger. But to prepare for this, take time to answer the following questions.

Insight Questions

1. My last incident with anger was _____

   _____

2. I reacted by ( ) Yelling ( ) Throwing ( ) Hitting ( ) Keeping silent ( ) Walking away ( ) Leaving the house ( ) Crying ( ) Talking to others ( ) Other _____

   _____

3. I usually react to my emotion of anger by _____

   _____

   _____

4. The circumstances or factors that led to my last incident with anger were _____

   _____

   _____

5. I overreacted by _____

   _____

6. The focus of my anger was _____

   _____

7. As I reflect on the incident, I believe the real issue was

   _____

   _____

8. I need to talk to _____ about the real issue that was bothering me.

9. I need to apologize to _____ for my actions of

   _____

10. With regard to swearing ( ) I do not swear at all ( ) I swear only inside (to myself) ( ) I am swearing more inside than

before ( ) I swear inside and in front of others ( ) I am swearing out loud more than before ( ) Others have talked to me about my swearing.

11. If I am honest with myself, I think my swearing is really my trying to express the emotion of _____

    _____

    toward _____

12. I could better express the above emotion by _____

    _____

    _____rather than by swearing.

13. I would like to do the following about my swearing:

    _____

    _____

8.

Outside Help for Anger

When I arrived, I could still see the flashing lights of the police car and the ambulance. A crowd had gathered even though it was late at night. I got out of my car and started toward the house. As I approached the front porch, two policemen emerged from the house with Ralph in handcuffs. As Ralph looked up and saw me, he cried, "You've got to help me! You've got to help me!" I really didn't have time to respond, because the policemen shoved him into their patrol car and drove away.

Ralph had lost his temper, beaten his wife, and slapped his children around. His wife almost died. A neighbor heard the yelling and called the police.

Ralph needs help. He needs to deal with his anger.

We all need to deal with our anger. "But I don't yell and throw things and hit people," you say. This may be true, but what about all the other, subtle expressions of anger?

An Anger Thermometer is illustrated to help us visualize some of the various forms or expressions of anger. You will notice that there are passive expressions and active expressions. The passive expressions are usually feelings of irritation that lie inside us. Active expressions usually involve objects or other people and are outside us. We are responsible for both the active and the passive expressions.

You may respond, "I have tried to control my temper, but I just can't seem to master it. I keep blowing up. I need some help . . . I haven't been doing very well by myself."

Outside help is available. There is someone who can give us enough wisdom and strength to deal effectively with our emotions of anger. I mentioned earlier that anger is a God-

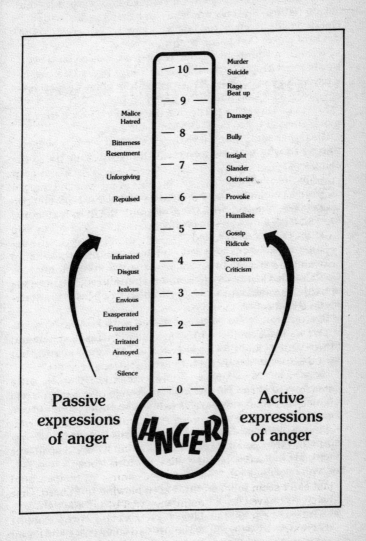

given emotion which has been clouded and warped by our old sin nature. The only one who can help us to deal with our emotions effectively is the one who gave us our emotions in the first place. God is the beginning place.

Recently a young man came home from college for a visit. He shared with his father the many things he had learned as a psychology major. His father asked him what his psychology professors said about the guilt complex.

He said, "Dad, this is the one thing they all have in common. They all try to deal with the guilt complex."

His father said, "Son, have they ever given you any suggestion as to why man is universally 'hung up' with the guilt complex?"

"Well, not really."

"Would you like to have your old dad tell you why man is universally 'hung up' with the guilt complex? In fact, you can even share this with your professors."

"What is the answer, dad?"

"It's simple," he responded. "It's because they're *guilty!*"

You may smile at this, but it's true. We have all missed God's mark. If there is any comfort in numbers, we have all sinned. "Yes, all have sinned; all fall short of God's glorious ideal" (Roman 3:23, LB).

It is not just Adam who missed God's mark. We've missed it personally. We've lied. We've stolen. We've taken the name of the Lord in vain. As we look at the Ten Commandments, we recognize instantly that we are guilty.

No one forced us to lie. No one made us steal. No one caused us to cheat. No one makes us angry. We sin because of our will. Some may say, "It is because of the sin nature." Pass the buck again.

Wait a minute! Did Adam have a sin nature when he sinned in the Garden of Eden? He lived in a perfect environment. He had a perfect heredity. No, with his own free will Adam chose to disobey God.

We shouldn't blame Adam for our sin. We can't say, "The devil made me do it." We have to face the issue squarely. We sin because we willfully choose to. The only way the guilt complex can be removed so that we can enjoy peace and joy is to realize against whom we have sinned. It is God.

The In-Spite-Of Love

Even with the offense of our sinful lives, God still loves us. Isn't that tremendous? In fact, God loved us so much that He sent His Son to live on this planet and identify with humanity. God Himself took on the physical form of a human being. He came with one purpose. He said, "I came that they may have life [spiritual life], and have it abundantly" (John 10:10, RSV).

> People are strange
> I cannot understand them.
> I had a sweetheart
> Who seemed to love me.
> I gave her roses, sweets, gems.
> I gave her all I had, my heart—
> And she broke it.
> I cannot forgive her
>
> God had a world
> That should have loved Him.
> He gave it beauty, light and life.
> He gave it all He had, His Son,
> And it crucified Him.
>
> People are strange
> I cannot understand them.
> But God—
> He loved them.
>
> *Earl Marlatt*

Poisoned Meat

For us to enjoy daily peace and joy in our lives we must first experience peace with God. This is done by personally inviting Jesus Christ to come and live in our lives. This is an act of faith.

Many people believe faith is just a religious word, but this is not true. We live our entire lives by faith. We have faith that the butcher won't sell us poisoned meat. We have faith that the person driving an oncoming car will stay in his own lane.We have faith that the druggist is putting the right pills in our prescription bottle. We have faith that when we turn on the faucet, water will come out. Life on this planet is lived by faith. In many cases, it is blind faith.

Yellow Butter

Some people remark, "I will never believe in Christ, because I don't understand all there is to know about God."

We don't have to know everything about God in order to have a personal experience with Christ. Do we understand all there is to know about how a black-and-white cow can eat green grass and turn it into white milk and yellow butter? Yet we can enjoy the end result even though we don't understand the process.

I have dealt with many men and women who have had an intellectual encounter with Christ. They know truths about Him. Some even get a little emotional about the teachings of Jesus. Yet they never have personally received Christ at a point in time.

Are You Married?

I have asked many people, "Do you know Christ as your personal Savior?" Some respond by saying, "I hope so" or "I think so" or "I'm trying."

When someone answers with a shade of doubt, I simply say, "Ask me if I am married."

This usually catches the person off-guard. He or she says, "What?"

"Ask me if I am married!"

I respond, "I hope so" or "I think so" or "I'm trying."

No, my friend, when we are married, we *know so!* When we receive Christ, there is no doubt. We know so!

Have you received Christ by faith? Do you know that your sins are forgiven? Can you remember a time when you made this commitment?

If not, you probably do not know Christ. But you are not alone in this situation. As I travel from church to church, I meet many who have only a head knowledge and not a heart knowledge of Christ.

Could you be in the same situation? If so, how about making that decision now? You do not have to bow your head. You can make this decision with your eyes wide open.

In Romans 10:9-10 we read: "For if you tell others with your own mouth that Jesus Christ is your Lord, and believe in your own heart that God has raised him from the dead, you will be saved. For it is by believing in his heart that a man becomes right with God; and with his mouth he tells others of his faith, confirming his salvation" (LB).

Are you willing to tell others that Jesus is your Lord? Do you believe God raised Jesus from the dead? If so, then you are saved, according to the Word of God.

Gigantic Goose Pimple

You may say, "But I don't feel any different." Feelings do not count at this point. The important thing is an act of your will by faith. The feelings will come later. The following chart may help to illustrate this truth:

1. HEAR — FACTS — MIND

2. BELIEVE }
3. RECEIVE } FAITH — EMOTIONS

4. DOING — FEELINGS — WILL

Many people have become involved with numbers 1 and 2 and not with 3 and 4. There are two parts to true faith. I could show you a real five-hundred-dollar bill and tell you I will give it to you (1). You could even believe it is real (2) and still not have it. It is only when you mix your belief and faith and receive it that it becomes yours (3). Then the feelings will come (4).

People have said to me, "If I could only feel the way you do about God, then I would believe." This is putting the cart before the horse. This is like saying, "If I could feel as if I owned five hundred dollars, then I would believe it." No, first comes the twofold step of faith.

Many are plagued with doubt about their decision for Christ. They have not felt real assurance that they are saved. This is usually because they are told by others that they should have some great emotional experience. To most people, this does not happen. When they read stories or hear of others who have some "gigantic spiritual goose pimple," they feel left out. They wonder whether they are second-class Christians of some kind.

Satan is deceiving many today with this kind of thinking. There is no "instant spirituality." There is no "special gift" that sets us on a higher spiritual plane. God has placed us in Christ as joint heirs by an act of simple, childlike faith. It is simple as that, and man cannot change this fact.

What God Says

Listen to what God Himself says about the security that is yours in Christ Jesus, and then claim these promises for yourself:

"God has said, 'I will never, *never* fail you nor forsake you' " (Hebrews 13:5, LB).

"And what is it that God has said? That he has given us eternal life, and that this life is in his Son. So whoever has God's Son has life; whoever does not have his Son, does not have life. I have written this to you who believe in the Son of God so that you may know you have eternal life" (1 John 5:11–13, LB).

Jesus Himself declared:

"My sheep recognize my voice, and I know them, and they follow me. I give them eternal life and they shall never perish. No one shall snatch them away from me, for my Father has given them to me, and he is more powerful then anyone else, so no one can kidnap them from me. I and the Father are one" (John 10:27–30, LB).

Today, by faith, settle the issue of your salvation. Invite Christ into your life and seal your decision by claiming God's assurance. Then determine with God's help not to return to your old life and your old way of thinking and your old way of responding with anger.

A graphic presentation of these important truths is shown in the back of this book, beginning on page 174.

There Is a War Going On

The beginning place for dealing with anger effectively is a personal relationship with Christ. He will help us learn how to control and deal with this most important emotion.

Please do not misunderstand me at this point. Just because a person receives Christ does not guarantee that he or she will no longer have a problem with anger. As Christians, we do not have a "king's X" on problems; in fact, we may have a bigger problem. Before I was a Christian I could sin and enjoy it. I could tell people off and rant and rave and really get into my anger. Now that I am a Christian, God's Holy Spirit convicts me through the Word of God and my conscience that those actions are not godly responses. There is a battle going on inside me.

Jerry began to weep in my office. He was a big man, but he seemed like a little boy. "I told her if she didn't like it, she could get out and stay out. I had said that many times before when we had an argument. Last week I said it again and she said, 'Ok, big boy! Whatever you say!' I know I shouldn't have said that. I know I am wrong. I'm a Christian, but I sure haven't been living like one. I've been livin' like the devil." Jerry's wife Lucille had had enough. She walked out on him and took the children. Jerry had a battle going on inside.

Paul the apostle describes this battle when he says, "I don't understand myself at all, for I really want to do what is right, but I can't. I do what I don't want to—what I hate. I know perfectly well that what I am doing is wrong, and my bad conscience proves that I agree with these laws I am breaking. But I can't help myself, because I'm no longer doing it. It is sin inside me that is stronger than I am that makes me do these evil things.

"I know I am rotten through and through so far as my old sinful nature is concerned. No matter which way I turn I can't make myself do right. I want to but I can't. When I want to do good, I don't; and when I try not to do wrong, I do it anyway. Now if I am doing what I don't want to, it is plain where the trouble is: sin still has me in its evil grasp.

"It seems to be a fact of life that when I want to do what is right, I inevitably do what is wrong. I love to do God's will so far as my new nature is concerned; but there is something else deep within me, in my lower nature, that is at war with my mind and wins the fight and makes me a slave to the sin that is still within me. In my mind I want to be God's willing servant but instead I find myself still enslaved to sin.

"So you see how it is: my new life tells me to do right, but the old nature that is still inside me loves to sin. Oh, what a terrible predicament I'm in! Who will free me from my slavery to this deadly lower nature? Thank God! It has been done by Jesus Christ our Lord. He has set me free" (Romans 7:15–25).

"I advise you to obey only the Holy Spirit's instructions. He will tell you where to go and what to do, and then you won't always be doing the wrong things your evil nature wants you to. For we naturally love to do evil things that are just the opposite from the things that the Holy Spirit tells us to do; and the good things we want to do when the Spirit has his way with us are just the opposite of our natural desires. These two forces within us are constantly fighting each other to win control over us, and our wishes are never free from their pressures" (Galatians 5:16–17).

There is a struggle raging continually in our lives. It is the battle for the will—the will to do right. When a person receives Christ, he or she receives a new resource for doing right—a new resource for dealing with the emotion of anger.

In the following chapters we will look at many different ways to deal with anger. These techniques and suggestions will, however, be effective only as we allow Christ to control and guide through them. Before we examine these techniques, it is helpful to look at another strong influence on the emotion of anger . . . our basic temperament.

9.

Anger and Your Temperament

"I just don't understand myself," Judy said with tears streaming down her face. "Clyde said that he's had it. That he is through. He said he couldn't take any more of my perfectionism. Can I help it if I like a clean house and he is messy? I've always been neat and organized. No one else in the family seems to care."

What made Judy so tidy and Clyde so disorganized? Was it just the way they were raised? Was it just the different environments in which they grew up?

Numerous theories have been generated in an attempt to explain man's behavior. The ancients emphasized man's inherited traits as the cause for his actions. Freud and his followers blamed man's environment and childhood experiences. Actually, both contribute to our conduct, but our inherited temperament influences us most.

Through the genes at conception, man inherits from his parents and grandparents his entire nature, including the color of his hair, eyes, body structure, talents and, of course, his temperament. That temperament acts as the single most powerful influence on his behavior, for it is the cause of his spontaneous actions and reactions.

Occasionally some of the brainwashed victims of modern psychology try to accentuate the significance of "learned behavior," but I find this suggestion rather puzzling. Consider, for example, four children all raised in the same basic home environment and subjected to the same training principles. Will they all act the same? No, they will be as different as night and day! Something dissimilar in their inherited ingredients must have caused this. One will be neat and orderly, and one will be messy. One will dress in "grubbies" and casual clothes, and the other in dress-up styles and coordinated outfits. These and a host of other differences will appear in their lives long before their parents have a chance to teach such things.

The Four Basic Temperaments

Made up of the traits we inherit at conception, temperament is influenced later by childhood training, education, life experiences, environment, and both human and spiritual motivation.

The best theory of temperament was proposed by Hippocrates 2,400 years ago. He suggested that people fit into four basic categories: the sanguine super-extrovert salesman, the choleric extrovert strong-willed leader, the melancholy introvert perfectionist, and the phlegmatic super-introvert passivist. Although variations have been suggested, this theory is disseminated today very similar to its original form. Perhaps the key addition is that no one fits perfectly into one of Hippocrates' molds, for people tend to represent a blend of two or more of these temperaments. This seems to be a reasonable corollary, since they show physical characteristics of both the mother and father.

Most people tend to be predominantly one temperament with slight traits of another. It is not uncommon for a person to be 80 percent sanguine and 20 percent phlegmatic, or 70 percent choleric and 30 percent melancholic. There is no end of variations and percentages these traits may produce; one man I tested proved to be about 60 percent sanguine, 20 percent melancholy, and 20 percent phlegmatic.

Temperament and Transformed Temperaments

The analysis of human temperament is one of the most fascinating subjects I have ever studied. Although it is tempting to launch into a comprehensive discussion of it, I must deal with temperament here only as it relates to the problem of anger. For additional insights I suggest you read the following books: Spirit-Controlled Temperament, Transformed Temperaments, Understanding the Male Temperament, and How to Develop Your Child's Temperament.[1]

The Sanguine and Anger

The sanguine temperament breeds a warm, friendly, and outgoing person who draws people to himself like a magnet. He is a good talker, a happy-go-lucky optimist, the "life of the party." Though generous and compassionate, responsive to his surroundings and to the moods or feelings of others, like the other temperaments he features some natural weaknesses. He is often weak-willed, emotionally unstable and explosive, restless and egotistical. Voted "most likely to succeed" in his youth, he rarely measures up to expectations. He has great difficulty following through on details and is almost never quiet. Beneath his bold exterior he is often insecure and fearful. Sanguines make good salesmen, speakers, actors, and sometimes leaders.

A sanguine is rarely depressed in the company of others. He is such a response-oriented person that the sight of another individual usually lifts his spirits and brings a smile to his face. Whatever periods of depression he does experience almost invariably occur when he is alone.

Many undisciplined sanguines experience anger. Their lack of discipline and weakness of will has usually made them rather unproductive, much to their chagrin and self-disappointment. They are also prone to obesity because of their inability to refuse fattening desserts and other delicacies. This lowers their self-esteem and heightens their tendency toward angry expressions. Although they usually go through the motions of responding happily to other people, their tendency toward anger will increase. One writer likened them to Peter Pan . . . they wish never to grow up. Although they are well-liked and attractive, they are undependable and without real substance.

Sanguine individuals have a strong tendency to be disorganized and unproductive. You have probably heard about the sanguine businessman who rushed into the airport and up to the ticket counter and said, "Give me a ticket quick!" To which the clerk replied, "A ticket to where, sir?" "Anywhere," said the businessman. "I've got business all over."

Their anger is of the "hot-flash" variety. They can explode faster than any other temperament. One thing about their anger, though, is that once they have exploded, they forget all about it . . . *you* don't but *they* do. They rarely get ulcers . . . they give them to everyone else.

As these charming sanguines who often act like overgrown children become aware of their own shallowness, their insecurities are heightened. They become defensive, sensitive to slights or criticism, almost obsessed with others' opinions of them. It is not uncommon for them to become angry at this point. They may even blame their parents for indulging them so much in childhood that they never developed self-discipline, but it is very difficult for them to blame themselves, confess their sin, and seek the filling of the Holy Spirit for the strength of character they so desperately need.

If they do not face their problem realistically and learn to walk in the Spirit, they will fluctuate up and down between anger and happiness for a time until, in some childlike way, they make the mental adjustment and then go through life fixed in a playful position far beneath their level of potential.

Spirit-filled sanguines are different! The Holy Spirit convicts them that their angry thought patterns are sin, and guides them to those areas of productivity that make it easier for them to accept and appreciate themselves. When a sanguine is filled with the Spirit, like the apostle Peter in the Book of Acts, he or she becomes a productive and effective person not overwhelmed with anger.

The Choleric and Anger

The choleric temperament produces a practical activist. He is strong-willed, a natural leader, and very optimistic. His brain is filled with ideas, projects, or objectives, and he usually sees them through. Like Mr. Sanguine he is extrovert, but not nearly so intense. Although very productive in life, he reflects serious natural weaknesses. He is self-sufficient, impetuous, and hot-tempered, and he tends to be harsh or cruel. In fact, no one can be as cutting and sarcastic as a choleric. He makes a good supervisor, general, builder, crusader, politician, or organizer, but he is not usually able to do precise detail work.

The choleric rarely becomes depressed, primarily because his active, goal-conscious mind keeps him so motivated that he projects fourteen different programs simultaneously. If one of them proves baffling or frustrating, his disappointment is short-lived and he quickly pursues a fresh challenge. Cholerics are happy when busy, and thus they have little time to be depressed. Their primary frustration in life is that there are not enough hours in the day to engage in their endless supply of goals and objectives.

Cholerics have a strong will and are very determined individuals. You may recall the story of the sanguine man married to his choleric wife. One day she came to her husband and said, "Henry, I want to buy a pair of scissors."

Henry replied, "We can't afford them."

The conversation went on like this:

"But I want them."

"I said *no*!"

"But I need them."

"The answer is no."

"Henry, I *need* those scissors!"

Henry responded, "Woman, if you say one more word about those scissors, I am going to take you outside and dump you down into the well."

"Scissors," said the choleric wife.

Henry then jumped up, grabbed her, and took her outside to the well. "Woman, if you promise not to say one more word about scissors, I will not throw you down the well."

"SCISSORS!" she replied.

"Okay, you asked for it!" With that Henry tied a rope on his wife and lowered her into the well. When she was halfway down, he said, "If you promise not to say anything about scissors, I'll pull you back up."

"SCISSORS!" came the echo from the well.

"That did it!" said Henry. He let go of the rope, and his wife's head disappeared underwater. As Henry peered into the well, the only thing he could see was his choleric wife's hand sticking out of the water. The first two fingers of her hand were moving back and forth in a scissors-like motion. Choleric individuals are very strong-willed and determined.

The rejection or insults that often set off other temperaments into periods of depression never faze a choleric. He is so thick-skinned, self-sufficient, and independent by nature that he rarely feels the need for other people. Instead of feeling sorry for himself when alone, he spends the time originating new plans.

Emotionally he is the most underdeveloped of all the temperaments. For that reason he usually experiences very slight mood changes. Although he quickly becomes angry, he rarely indulges in self-pity. Instead, he explodes all over everyone else. Because he is so insensitive to a person's opinion of him, he is not vulnerable to depression brought on by others. If a choleric ever battles depression, it will come as a result of frustration or retreat.

Unless he achieves victory over his anger early in life, the choleric becomes a very hostile and bitter old man. He is unforgiving by nature and consequently usually has ulcers by the time he is forty years old. He is the one temperament that both gets and gives ulcers.

As a Christian, the choleric must learn to rest in the Lord and commit his way to Him. An indomitable will and spirit of self-sufficiency often cause him to be a useless, unproductive Christian because he insists on doing everything in the flesh instead of the Spirit. If he does successfully promote Christian activities, his pride makes him spiritually myopic and he fails to discern his carnal motivation.

The peace of the Holy Spirit that passes all understanding will modulate his thinking pattern, causing him to concentrate on the Lord first and then on the task. He must learn that God's program does not depend on him; rather, he needs to depend on God. He must further recognize that fulfilling the work of God is not enough; he must do it in the power of the Spirit. As the Bible says, "Not by might, nor by power, but by my spirit, saith the Lord of hosts" (Zechariah

4:6, KJV). The apostle Paul, possibly the best illustration of a Spirit-filled choleric used of God, had learned this well, for he said, "When I am weak, then am I strong" (2 Corinthians 12:10, KJV).

The flesh-filled choleric Christian can become angry until he realizes this principle, because he gets frustrated by the lack of spiritual results from his hard-driving, fleshly efforts. Instead of blaming himself for his carnal, self-willed spirit, he may swell up in self-pity and withdraw from his church activities.

A choleric's carnal spirit is often easily discerned by others in the congregation, and thus he may be bypassed when officers are elected. "I don't understand," he complains. "Isn't my hard work sufficient proof of my devotion to Christ?" Happy is the choleric who learns with James to say, "If the Lord will, we shall live, and do this, or that" (James 4:15, KJV). If he seeks the priorities of the will of God through the leading of the Holy Spirit in his life, he will be not only more productive, but also more composed. When once he comprehends that walking in the Spirit is the secret to spiritual productivity, he will gain consistency in his Christian life.

The ability of the Holy Spirit to transform a choleric tendency to anger is illustrated superbly in the life of the apostle Paul. If ever a man was an illustration of choleric temperament, it was Saul of Tarsus before he became a Christian, renamed Paul. After his conversion, his indomitable choleric will directed by the Holy Spirit surged forward throughout the events related in the Book of Acts.

Paul's response to confinement offers a classic illustration of circumstances overcome through the invasion of man's spiritual nature by the Holy Spirit. Confined to the cold, clammy Mamertine Prison in Rome for preaching the Gospel, he manifested not one sign of self-pity. Instead, this dynamic Christian took advantage of the opportunity to share his faith personally with every new Roman soldier assigned to him as a guard. So many of these men were converted that he addressed the church of Rome, "All the saints salute you, chiefly they that are of Caesar's household" (Philippians 4:22, KJV). In addition, from this prison he penned the prison epistles, including the epistle of joy called the letter to the Philippians, in which he stated, "I have learned, in whatsoever state I am, therewith to be content" (4:11, KJV). Even Spirit-filled cholerics can have victory over angry outbursts.

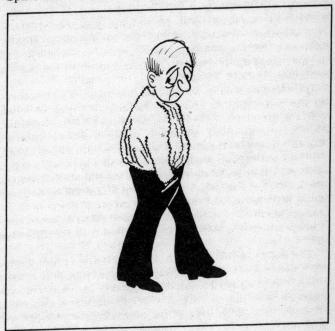

The Melancholy and Anger

The richest of all temperaments is the melancholy. Rich not only in gifts and esthetic appreciation, it has the capacity to experience the entire spectrum of emotional mood fluctuations. It is also rich in emotional weaknesses, particularly in the tendency to become angry and depressed. Some of the world's greatest geniuses have been gifted melancholies who squandered their talent in the slough of despondency, becoming apathetic and unproductive. This is so much in evidence that the ancients frequently used the words *melancholy* and *depression* interchangeably.

The melancholy is usually the most talented of all temperaments. A natural perfectionist, very sensitive and appreciative of the fine arts, he is analytical and self-sacrificing. As a rule he is not outgoing by nature and rarely pushes himself forward, but he makes a very faithful friend. However, he tends to be moody, critical, pessimistic, and self-centered. The world's great artists, composers, philosophers, inventors, and theoreticians have usually been melancholies.

Although everyone is vulnerable to his own thinking pattern, none is more responsive than the melancholy. Among his other creative gifts, he harbors a great ability to suggest images to the screen of his imagination—probably in living color with stereophonic sound. Because melancholies are moody by nature, they may regard their moods as spontaneous, but it has been learned that moods result directly from thinking patterns. If a melancholy guards his thought processes and refuses to indulge in the mental sins of anger, resentment, self-persecution, and self-pity, he will not yield to his predisposition toward depression.

One day several friends and I were dining in a restaurant. Suddenly a melancholy college-aged man with a gaunt look appeared at the edge of our table and asked, "Pardon me, but may I ask you folks if you were laughing at me?" Naturally we were shocked into silence. Finally I said, "Young man, I don't think we've ever seen you before in our lives." With that he excused himself and walked away. Reflecting on the incident, we concluded that during our laughter and conversation, we must have looked in his direction, which gave this troubled young man the impression that we were laughing at his expense. Equally as substantial are many of the depression-causing events in the life of the average melancholy.

Melancholy Perfectionists

Melancholies often are easily depressed because they are perfectionists. Most people could profit by having more perfectionist tendencies, but the true perfectionist is made miserable by them. In the first place, he measures himself by his own arbitrary standard of perfection and becomes discouraged with himself when he falls short. The fact that his standard is usually so high that neither he nor anyone else could live by it rarely occurs to him. Instead, he insists that his criterion for perfection is "realistic."

In addition to perfectionism he also is very conscientious and prides himself on being "dependable" and "accurate." Naturally all of his friends fall short of this standard, so it is not uncommon for him to become angry about himself and his associates. Very rigid and inflexible, he finds it difficult to tolerate the slightest deviation from what he considers to be the measure of excellence.

Such perfectionist-prone melancholies can love their children dearly while at the same time becoming angry with them. Children are notoriously disorganized and unpredictable; they follow their own schedules and insist on acting like children. A rigid melancholy parent finds it difficult to cope with such unpredictability and consequently may experience anger. Sometimes a melancholy mother may become ambivalent, loving her children intensely while at the same time being filled with anger and bitterness toward them. The carefree, happy-go-lucky tyke who insists on trekking across the clean kitchen floor in muddy boots can be a source of irritation to any mother, particularly to a melancholy. Before she was married, she probably could not retire for the night until her shoes were lined up properly and the bathroom was in perfect order. Children automatically change that, but perfectionists find it difficult to cope with such change; consequently, depression is their outlet. They become angered at the lack of perfection in others and indulge in self-pity because they are the only ones striving for lofty goals. Such thought patterns invariably produce anger.

In fairness to melancholy people, we note that they are as critical of themselves as they are of others. Consequently they tend to develop an inadequate view of themselves. From early childhood they construct a disparaging self-image on the screen of their imagination. As they get older, they tend to reject themselves even more, unlike some of the other temperaments who learn to accept themselves. If they were permitted to verbalize their criticisms in childhood, they are apt to be verbally critical in adulthood. Each time they indulge in oral criticism, they only embed the spirit of criticism more deeply in their mind, and critics are never happy people!

One day I had an opportunity to see this principle in action. As I was passing through the security screening before boarding a plane, the security officer was criticizing the individuals who flew on that airline as "slovenly, inconsiderate, disorganized, and ungrateful people." I took it just about as long as I could, but finally, looking at him with a big smile (I find one can say almost anything if he smiles), I observed, "You must be an unhappy man!"

He looked at me rather startled and replied, "Why do you say that?"

"Because you're so critical. I've never met a happy person who is a critical person."

After inspecting my baggage, the officer said, "Thank you, sir, I needed that." To my amazement he turned to the next customer and said, "Hello, how are you? So glad to have you on our airline."

I don't know how long the officer will profit from that experience, but I am certain he is capable of making himself happy or miserable in direct proportion to the way he thinks of and talks to people.

Self-Sacrifice and Persecution-Proneness

Two characteristics of the melancholy short-circuit each other: the natural desire to be self-sacrificing and the self-persecution tendency. Unless the melancholy is careful, this conflict will likely make a martyr out of him. Ordinarily he chooses the most difficult and trying location to ply his vocation. When others seem to be more successful or gain more renown, instead of facing realistically the fact that he has chosen the path of self-sacrifice, he indulges in self-pity because his journey winds uphill and leads through arduous straits.

Melancholies rarely explode—at first. That is, if you insult a melancholy, he will usually react properly at the time. But after you're gone he will mull it over, stew about it, and become upset. When you see him two months later, long after you have forgotten the experience, he may "blow up" just at the sight of you. Melancholies have a slow-burning fuse that is very long.

The determination of a melancholy to gripe and criticize merely compounds his negative thinking, perpetuates his anger, and ultimately brings him to despair. For this reason 1 Thessalonians 5:18 can come to his rescue. If he painstakingly and consistently follows its formula, he will never become depressed: "In everything give thanks: for this is the will of God in Christ Jesus concerning you" (KJV).

Melancholy Creativity

Fortunately for the melancholy, he possesses an unusual creative ability to project all kinds of images on the screen of his imagination. Once he fully realizes that positive feelings are the direct result of constructing wholesome mental images of himself and his circumstances, he is well on the road to recovery and prevention of future bouts with anger. Melancholy people risk anger primarily because of the continual misuse of their creative imagination. That is, on the imagination screen of their mind they project negativism, hurt, self-pity, helplessness, and despair. When they realize that their creative suggestions can work either for or against them, they can carefully project only those images that are pleasing to God. Such thoughts will lift their spirits, stabilize their moods, and help them to avoid anger.

The Phlegmatic and Anger

The easygoing, never-get-upset "nice guy" is the phlegmatic. Besides featuring a calm and likable disposition, Mr. Phlegmatic is a cheerful fellow who works well with other people, an efficient, conservative, dependable, witty person with a practical turn of mind. Since he is quite introvert, as a rule, his weaknesses like his strengths are not so readily perceptible as those of other temperaments. His most obvious weakness is a lack of motivation. He can ignore work graciously and is prone to be stubborn, stingy, and indecisive. His ability to look at life through the eyes of a spectator may generate a tendency to avoid "getting involved" with anything. Phlegmatics make good diplomats, since they are natural peacemakers. Many are teachers, doctors, scientists, comedians, and editors. When externally motivated, they make very capable leaders.

Generally a phlegmatic person is not easily angered. He usually has such a high boiling point that he will seldom be explosive, though he may burn red inside. His unique sense of humor signals a happy outlook on life, and rarely does he reflect much mood fluctuation in either direction. It is possible to know a phlegmatic all his life and never see him truly angry, for no matter what the occasion, he tends to mentally excuse the person who has offended, injured, or rejected him. His ability to adjust to unpleasant circumstances is unbelievable to the other three temperaments, which find it easy to gripe or criticize mentally and verbally.

If a phlegmatic ever does display anger, it is usually aimed at his own lack of aggressiveness. Many times his practical, capable mind devises a suitable plan of action for a given set of circumstances, but because of his passive inclination or his fear of being criticized by others, he keeps it to himself.

Consequently, driven by family or other group pressure, he may find himself pursuing a plan inferior to his own. This can produce irritation which, when followed by self-pity, will make him angry. His anger is usually short-lived, however, because before long someone will come along who will amuse and entertain him.

There is one critical period in life when the phlegmatic is most vulnerable to anger. During the fifth or sixth decade he often becomes aware that the other temperaments have passed him by vocationally, spiritually, and in every other way. While he was passively watching the game of life as a spectator, his more aggressive friends were stepping through the doors of opportunity. His security-mindedness has checked him from attending upon daring adventures in life, and thus his existence may seem rather stale to him during this period. If he indulges in self-pity, he will definitely become angry.

Instead of blaming his fear or indolence, he finds it much easier to reproach "society" or "the breaks" or "my luck." Such a person should learn from the Lord Jesus early in life to attempt great things for God, for Christ said, "According to your faith be it unto you" (Matthew 9:29, KJV).

The Remedy for Temperament Weakness

God has a thrilling plan for overcoming all temperament weaknesses—even anger. In Ephesians 5:18 He designates it as being continually "filled with the Spirit." The filling of the Holy Spirit produces three great emotional characteristics:

1. A song in the heart (Ephesians 5:19);
2. A thanksgiving mental attitude (Ephesians 5:20);
3. A submissive spirit (Ephesians 5:21).

It is impossible to be angry when all three of these emotions are present. The filling of the Spirit, therefore, is the obvious remedy for the emotion of anger.

When Christians walk in the Spirit, they will maintain the proper mental attitude so that they can respond in praise and thanksgiving to the negative circumstances of life. Remember, God has promised not to permit negative circumstances above our ability to cope with them. He is, of course, presupposing that we maintain the proper mental attitude.

Several components make up the right mental attitude. Consider them carefully to see if you possess them.

1. Complete commitment to the will and way of God (Romans 6:11–13; 12:1–2). Circle the percent of commitment you feel that you have at this point in your life.

   10% 20% 30% 40% 50% 60% 70% 80% 90% 100%

2. Knowledge of the principles of God (Romans 12:2). No one will know perfectly all the principles of God for living, but you can daily refresh your mind on them by reading and studying the Word of God. I study the Bible ( ) Every day (1) Several times a week ( ) A couple of times a month ( ) Rarely ( ) Never.

3. Faith (Romans 14:23; Hebrews 11:6). It is impossible to enlist the dynamic dimensions of God into your life without faith. If your faith is weak, don't wait for some miracle to make it strong. The following steps will strengthen your faith.

   a. Hear, read, and study the Bible (Romans 13:10).
   b. Pray for increased faith (1 Corinthians 12:31).
   c. Walk in the Spirit (Galatians 5:22–23).
   d. Experience faith (Romans 1:17) Each time you trust God for something, it is easier to trust Him the next time. I would like to trust God for the following:

   _____

   _____

   _____

   _____

   _____

   _____

10.

Is It Ever Right to Be Angry?

"I feel so guilty," said Carla. "I have all these angry feelings inside me, and I know that they are bad. I know the Bible says it is wrong to get angry, but I am angry! I know the Bible says to forgive, but I just can't do it! It's not fair what they did to me!"

Carla is not alone in her feelings. At some point in our lives, we all have experienced them.

The question then comes, Is it ever right to be angry? Are there situations and circumstances in which anger is legitimate? Is it possible to be angry and not be sinning at the same time? Can a "born-again," "Spirit-filled" Christian be angry and still be walking with God? Some people believe that all anger is sin. But how can we reconcile the Bible verses that tell us to stop being angry, not to seek revenge, to avoid those who are angry, and not to harbor resentment with the apostle Paul's words, "Be angry and sin not"? It is not a small problem; many dedicated, godly men and women struggle with this.

Carla's story will help to illustrate this dilemma. It is one of the most tragic I have ever heard in my counseling. As a very young child she overheard a conversation which revealed that the person she thought was her father was not. Being so young, the only thing she knew to do was to cry. With the passage of time, she repressed the hurt she felt.

When Carla was seven, she spent the summer with an aunt and uncle. It was not a happy time. There were angry words from the couple. Uncle Sid would slap her in the face and beat her with a belt.

Then several weeks into the summer, it happened. One day Uncle Sid slapped her around and in his anger shouted, "I'll show you not to obey me!" He ripped off her dress and raped her. After that he did it often.

Later in the summer Uncle Sid brought his son into the room to watch as he raped Carla—he wanted to give him "first-hand sex education." Then Uncle Sid forced his son to have relations with her.

Sid still wasn't through with her. One day he made Carla put on her favorite dress and go with him "to visit some people." At the time Carla couldn't understand why Sid took along a second dress. She was also wondering who they were going to visit.

Sid took Carla to a business office. The two men they met there tore her clothes and raped her in the office. One of the men had a camera and took pictures of all that went on.

It was not until Carla was an adult that she discovered the truth: "Uncle Sid" was not her uncle, but her father.

Carla is angry. In fact, when I heard her story, I became angry. I felt helpless, as she did. There was nothing either of us could do to change what had happened in her past. But where does she go from here? Does Carla have a right to be angry? Is her anger sin? Is the anger I felt sin?

Archibald Hart addresses this point in his book *Feeling Free* when he says, "The need to differentiate between anger (the feeling) and hostility/aggression (the behavior arising out of the feeling) is even more important when we turn to understanding the New Testament's approach to the problem of anger. The Apostle Paul presents us with what at first seems to be an impossible paradox: 'Be ye angry, and sin not; let not the sun go down upon your wrath' (Ephesians 4:26).

"How can one be angry and sin not? The New English Bible translation makes a little clearer what the Apostle Paul was saying and provides us with a very up-to-date understanding not only of the nature of anger but also of its solution: 'If you are angry, do not let anger lead you into sin; do not let sunset find you still nursing it. . . .'

"My understanding of what Paul is saying here is that it is not the anger itself (as feeling) that is wrong, but that anger has the potential for leading you into sin. The point is that it is the translation or conversion of anger feelings into aggressive and hostile acts that leads us into sin. To feel anger, to tell someone that you feel angry, and to talk about your anger are both healthy and necessary. As long as you recognize the anger as your own and avoid hurting back the object of your anger, you are keeping it as a feeling—and all feelings are legitimate! What you do with your feeling may not be, and this is where you can fall into sin!"[1]

Moses and Anger

In her book *To Anger, With Love,* Elizabeth Skoglund writes concerning the verse "Be angry, and sin not": "Clearly anger is not sinful; yet how anger is handled may or may not be sinful. In Ephesians the key seems to be 'get over it quickly.' Anyone familiar with psychosomatic illness would admit that anger held in and kept is a destructive, negative emotion which can cause physical illness. That quiet man who never retaliates when his wife nags at him may not be so godly as unable to face and handle anger, and he may be a perfect candidate for a heart attack or stroke in a few years. He would be better off to face his anger and 'get over it quickly,' which can only be done through some kind of outward expression.

"The Bible is full of examples of anger—constructive and destructive. Probably God was first in the biblical record to feel anger when he expelled Adam and Eve from the Garden of Eden.

"In the Old Testament the life of Moses provides graphic illustrations of the biblical view of constructive and destructive ways of handling anger. At one point in his leadership of Israel, Moses failed to calm a rebellion in the camp of the Israelites after they had left Egypt to go to the land God had promised. Some of the men accused Moses, saying, 'You brought us out of lovely Egypt to kill us here in this terrible wilderness' (Numbers 16:13). Keeping in mind that in 'lovely Egypt' they had been slaves of the king, beaten and mistreated, it is no wonder Moses responded in anger: 'Then Moses was very angry and said to the Lord, "Do not accept their sacrifices!" ' (Num. 16:15).

"To Moses' surprise, God's anger outdid his: 'Get away

from these people so that I may instantly destroy them'
(Num. 16:21).

"At that point Moses pleaded to God: 'Must you be angry
with all the people when one man sins?' (Num. 16:22). And
God relented.

"None of this anger was sin; yet both Moses and God were
angry and free in expressing that anger.

"In contrast to Moses' good handling of anger in this situation is the time when Moses out of anger went against God.
God said to Moses, ' "Take the elders of Israel with you and
lead the people out to Mt. Horeb. I will meet you there at the
rock. Strike it with your rod—the same one you struck the
Nile with—and water will come pouring out, enough for
everyone!" Moses did as he was told, and the water gushed
out!' (Exod. 17:5–6).

"Later, however, the Israelites were again complaining
that there was not enough water to drink. 'A great mob
formed, and they held a protest meeting. . . . "You have deliberately brought us into this wilderness to get rid of us,
along with our flocks and herds. Why did you ever make us
leave Egypt?" ' (Num. 20:2–5).

"Reacting properly, Moses once again turned to God with
his dilemma, and God once again instructed him how to get
water. But this time Moses was clearly not to strike the rock
but to speak to it.

"With seeming calm Moses got the rod and called the
people as God had instructed him. Then in a burst of anger,
Moses said: ' "Listen you rebels! Must we bring you water
from this rock?" Then Moses lifted the rod and struck the
rock twice, and water gushed out; and the people and their
cattle drank' (Num. 20:10–22).

"However, the result in Moses' life was condemnation from
God. In his anger he had ignored God's command and struck
the rock—not only once but twice. It was an act which many
commentators feel has deep theological significance in biblical typology and thus a serious offence. Consequently, Moses
was deprived of the ultimate privilege of leading the Israelites
into the promised land although he was allowed to see it at a
distance.

"The obvious teaching regarding anger in the life of Moses

is that anger in itself is not wrong; nor is expressing anger wrong. It is the mode of expression that is important."[2]

Charles Swindoll makes the observation in his book *Three Steps Forward, Two Steps Back* that "anger is not necessarily sinful. God says, 'Be angry, and yet do not sin.' Not every expression of anger is wrong. It's as though I were to say to one of my children, 'Now, when you go out tonight, enjoy yourself. Really have a good time. But don't misuse your humor.' Or it's like the Lord when He says, 'I want you to love, but don't love the world. Don't even love the things of the world. I want you to love, but restrict that love to certain things.' This is the same thought. Be angry, but don't carry that anger to the point where it becomes sin."[3]

God's Anger

The Bible has much to say about God's anger and man's anger. There are major differences between them.

God's Anger	Man's Anger
Controlled, with purpose	Uncontrolled, without patience
Not with hatred, malice, or resentment	With hatred, malice, and resentment
Not selfish	Selfish
As an expression of concern	As an expression of indignation
To correct or curtail destructive behavior	To destroy the individual
As an expression of care	As an expression of revenge
Not to break relationships	To break relationships, to hurt
At injustice	At violations of self
At willful disobedience	At those who cross me

God's anger is different from man's, because it imposes holy wrath upon sin. It is wrong to compare our Lord's anger toward sin with man's anger, for Christ had a divine nature of holiness that man does not share; thus He could sustain a holy wrath without sin. His most severe anger involved righteous indignation against sin, never a response to personal rejection, insult, or injury.

Ephesians 4:26 states, "Be ye angry, and sin not: let not the sun go down upon your wrath." Since this is the only biblical text that seems to condone anger, we ought to examine it carefully. It carries two serious qualifications.

Notice: "Be ye angry" . . . (1) "and sin not:" (2) "let not the sun go down upon your wrath" (KJV).

The first qualification certainly limits anger: "Sin not"! It forbids any sinful thought or sinful expression of anger. Frankly, people never visit my counseling room with emotional distress from that kind of anger, because "righteous indignation" (my term for anger without sin) does not create hang-ups. And the second constraint obviously demands that this innocent anger not linger past sundown. Those who terminate their anger at sundown will not cultivate emotional problems either. Incidentally, verse 27 suggests that if innocent anger is permitted to burn past sundown, it "gives place to the devil."

On the other hand the Bible has much to say about unrighteous anger. Consider these Bible verses carefully:

Cease from anger, and forsake wrath. *Psalm 37:8*

Be not hasty in thy spirit to be angry: for anger resteth in the bosom of fools. *Ecclesiastes 7:9*

Better is a dinner of herbs where love is, than a stalled ox and hatred therewith. *Proverbs 15:17*

Better is a dry morsel, and quietness therewith, than an house full of sacrifices with strife. *Proverbs 17:1*

It is better to dwell in the wilderness, than with a contentious and angry woman. *Proverbs 21:19*

A wrathful man stirreth up strife: but he that is slow to anger appeaseth strife. *Proverbs 15:18*

He that hath no rule over his own spirit is like a city that is broken down, and without walls. *Proverbs 25:28*

Make no friendship with an angry man; and with a furious man thou shalt not go: lest thou learn his ways, and get a snare to thy soul. *Proverbs 22:24–25*

He that is slow to anger is better than the mighty; and he that ruleth his spirit than he that taketh a city. *Proverbs 16:32*

He that hideth hatred with lying lips, and he that uttereth a slander, is a fool. *Proverbs 10:18*

Hatred stirreth up strifes: but love covereth all sins. *Proverbs 10:12*

But now ye also put off all these; anger, wrath, malice, blasphemy, filthy communication out of your mouth.   *Colossians 3:8*

Wherefore, my beloved brethren, let every man be swift to hear, slow to speak, slow to wrath: for the wrath of man worketh not the righteousness of God.   *James 1:19–20, all KJV*

The solution to the apparent conflict between the thirteen verses that condemn anger and Ephesians 4:26, which seems to condone it, is really quite simple. The Bible permits righteous indignation and condemns all selfishly induced anger. You experience righteous indignation when you see an injustice perpetrated on another. For example, when a bully picks on a child, you feel a surge of emotion (righteous indignation) and go to the aid of the child. You do not sin in this, nor is it difficult to forget such externally induced anger after dark. But when someone rejects, insults, or injures you, that is a different matter. Is your emotion without sin? And do you forget it after dark?

The Lord Jesus' earthly expressions of anger provide another example. When He drove the moneychangers from the temple, His action was impersonal: "You have made my Father's house a den of thieves" (see Matthew 21:13). His anger toward the Pharisees later was kindled because they were spiritual "wolves" leading the sheep astray, not because they were hurting Him. In fact, when He was spat upon and nailed to a cross, He showed absolutely no anger. Instead we hear those familiar words, "Father, forgive them; for they know not what they do" (Luke 23:34, KJV). Our Lord never showed selfishly induced anger.

Those who use Ephesians 4:26 to justify the human frailty of anger tend to overlook an important fact. Just five verses on in that same context we read:

Let all bitterness, and wrath, and anger, and clamour, and evil speaking, be put away from you, with all malice: And be ye kind one to another, tenderhearted, forgiving one another, even as God for Christ's sake hath forgiven you.

Ephesians 4:31–32, KJV

It is quite clear from all this that righteous indignation is acceptable, but personally induced sin is wrong. What is the difference? Selfishness! Selfishly induced anger, which is the kind most of us experience and which causes so much personal and family havoc, is a terrible sin. That is why Scripture says, "Let all bitterness and wrath [all] and anger [all] be put away from you."

Let's come back to Carla for a moment. I think we can safely say that the anger she feels is justified. We can even call it righteous indignation. I think we could even say the anger I felt about the situation was legitimate. "If that is true, then there shouldn't be any problem," you may say. But there is.

The problem lies in what Carla is going to do about her past violation. She has a choice as to what to do with her righteous anger. You see, if she carries the anger too long (the sundown concept) it stands a strong possiblity of souring into resentment, bitterness, and hatred. What was healthy anger in the first place can grow malignant. Anger that at first was justified can be twisted into small little toeholds for the devil to come in and destroy emotional stability in Carla. And not only in Carla's life, but in your life and mine.

We have all been hurt by others at some time in our lives. Like Carla, we are victims—victims of man's inhumanity to man. How we react to these hurts and disappointments will mean the difference between emotional health and emotional ill-health, between spiritual health and spiritual ill-health.

I believe that the biggest single factor for emotional and spiritual health and for the elimination of the "malignant yeast" of anger is found in *forgiveness*. In the next chapter we will examine the importance of forgiveness and why it is so difficult to forgive those who have hurt us.

11.

Anger and Forgiveness

"I'm through. I've lost just about everything," Jay told me. "I invested my savings and hocked my house to get into the business, and now it's over. I trusted the other partners because they were all Christians . . . but I've been 'ripped off.' Now all the creditors are coming to me to pay the bills, and everyone in town thinks I am a crook, because the project failed. I'm so mad at Don and Fred I could spit nails!"

Does Jay's story sound familiar? Does it resemble your story? Have you been hurt financially, socially, and emotionally like Jay? Then join the club: hurt is "in" this year. "But I'm not hurting," you reply. If not, beware! Hurt is coming: you are not exempt from pain.

If we all experience situations of misunderstanding, hurt, pain, and suffering, why do some people handle it better than others? Why do some become angry and bitter and cynical about life and others who experience the same problems become happy, cheerful, and optimistic? I believe that much of the answer lies in forgiveness.

Forgive and Forget

Henry Ward Beecher (1813–1887), an American preacher once said, " 'I can forgive, but I cannot forget' is only another way of saying, 'I will not forgive.' Forgiveness ought to be like a cancelled note—torn in two, and burned up, so it never can be shown against one."

Beecher's thoughts were later modified by others to express, "If you haven't really forgotten, then you haven't truly forgiven." I believe that is a lie! I don't think we ever truly forget the offenses that we have experienced in life. I believe we remember them.

In fact, I don't think God forgets our offenses. "Wait a minute," you say. "What about the verse in Jeremiah 31:34 that says, '. . . Declares the Lord, "for I will forgive their iniquity, and their sin I will remember no more" '?" (NASB).

The phrase "I will remember no more" does not mean it is out of God's memory banks. How can an omniscient God—a God who knows everything—forget? Moreover, in other passages of Scripture God says He will remember their iniquities.

I believe the concept that God wants to convey is not that the event or sin itself is forgotten, but that judgment for the offense is removed. In other words, "I will not hold it against them in judgment anymore."

Many people struggle with the fact that they still remember the offenses that have occurred. How does one erase from the memory a divorce, a son or daughter on drugs, relatives who show favoritism to children other than your own, or the drunken driver who kills your mate? I don't forget being in jail or a concentration camp. I don't forget war. I don't forget that the next-door neighbor accidentally shot my son. I don't forget that I lost $10,000 in an investment that went sour because of the poor advice of a friend.

The plain truth of the matter is that I *do* remember. I *don't* forget! But I have a choice as to how I will respond to my memories. I can let my memories lie and move on in life, or I can let my memories overpower me.

William Blake illustrates this thought in his poem "A Poison Tree":

> I was angry with my friend:
> I told my wrath, my wrath did end.
> I was angry with my foe:
> I told it not, my wrath did grow.

Dying Grass

I can keep up the image. I can smile. I can act friendly. I can hide the fact that I really don't forget . . . but deep inside me is the burning fire of memory.

We have all learned how to cover and hide our hurts, disappointments, and anger. Eventually, however, the hurts, disappointments, and anger will surface.

I am reminded of the story of the minister and the deacon playing golf. Both were having a terrible time. Every time the deacon's ball went into the rough or off the course, he would swear. When the minister's ball went in the sand pit or into the water, he just smiled and said nothing. Finally the deacon said, "That's what I appreciate about you. When your ball goes off the fairway or into the water you just smile."

"That may be true," said the minister. "But where I spit the grass dies."

Is the grass dying near you? Are you struggling at present with a very real hurt? Are you wondering if there is any release available? Are you wondering if there is victory?

Why Is Forgiveness So Difficult?

Have you ever wondered why forgiveness is so difficult? It is basically because—

The person who is hurt (the offended party) does the forgiving and not the person being forgiven (the offender).

David Augsburger addresses this thought in his excellent book *The Freedom of Forgiveness* when he writes, "The man who forgives pays a tremendous price—the price of the evil he forgives!

"If the state pardons a criminal, society bears the burden of the criminal's deed.

"If I break a priceless heirloom that you treasure and you forgive me, you bear the loss and I go free.

"Suppose I ruin your reputation. To forgive me, you must freely accept the consequences of my sin and let me go free!

"In forgiveness, you bear your own anger and wrath at the sin of another, voluntarily accepting responsibility for the hurt he has inflicted on you.

"Myron Augsburger stated,

To forgive is costly. To forgive . . . is to carry one's own wrath on the sin of another; the guilty one is released, the offended one frees him, by bearing his own indignation and resolving it in love. God forgives by carrying His own wrath on the sin we've expressed against him . . . He absorbs our guilt and makes us free. Forgiveness goes through the sin to freedom.

"Forgiveness is costly because it is *substitutional*.

" 'All forgiveness, human and divine, is in the very nature of the case vicarious, substitutional,' writes James Buswell, Jr., 'and this is one of the most valuable views my mind has ever entertained. No one ever really forgives another, except he bears the penalty of the other's sin against him.'

"This substitution was perfectly expressed in Jesus Christ. Jesus Christ substituted Himself for us, bearing His own wrath, His own indignation at our sin. That's what forgiveness costs!"[1]

Forgiveness is very costly. It costs you, not the person being forgiven. Forgiveness means that justice will not always be fulfilled. Forgiveness does not rebuild the house that has been burned down by someone carelessly playing with matches. Forgiveness does not always put a broken marriage back together. Forgiveness does not restore virginity to the rape victim.

Forgiveness is letting go. It is the relaxation of your "death grip" on the pain you feel. Archibald Hart says,

"Forgiveness is surrendering my right to hurt you back if you hurt me."

David Augsburger goes on to say, "Forgiveness seems too easy. There should be blood for blood. Eye for eye.

"Yes, you can knock out a tooth for a tooth in retaliation, but what repayment can you demand from the man who has broken your home or betrayed your daughter or ruined your reputation?

"So few sins can be paid for, and so very seldom does the victim possess the power or the advantage to demand payment.

"In most cases, 'making things right' is beyond possibility! Repayment is impossible!

"So, here's where revenge comes in. If you cannot get equal payment or restitution out of the man who's wronged you, at least you can get revenge. Pay him back in kind, tit for tat. Serve him the same sauce.

" 'Get even' with him—if you insist. But remember, to get even you make yourself even with your enemy. You bring yourself down to his level, and below.

"There is a saying that goes, 'Doing an injury puts you

below your enemy; avenging an injury makes you but even with him; forgiving it sets you above him!'

"Revenge not only lowers you to your enemy's level; what's worse, it boomerangs. The man who seeks revenge is like the man who shoots himself in order to hit his enemy with the kick of the gun's recoil.

"Revenge is the most worthless weapon in the world. It ruins the avenger while more firmly confirming the enemy in his wrong. It initiates an endless flight down the bottomless stairway of rancor, reprisals and ruthless retaliation.

"Just as repayment is impossible, revenge is impotent!

" 'What? No repayment? No revenge? But I can have the soul-satisfaction of hating the wretch!'

"Well, yes, You can hate him. You can nurse a grudge until it grows into a full-blown hate, hooves, horns, tail and all.

"But what do you gain? In hatred, everybody loses!

"Hidden hatred can sour a likeable lady into a suspicious carper, a warm, understanding man into a caustic cynic.

"What does it cost to incubate hatred? It will cause a man to lose friends; a merchant to lose customers; a doctor, patients; an attorney, clients.

"In addition to corroding a disposition, harbored hatred can elevate blood pressure, upset disgestive works, ulcerate a stomach, or bring on a nervous breakdown. And ever hear of a coronary?

"Why boil inside? It's a form of slow suicide. Get all steamed up with resentment and an explosion is inevitable.

"And just simmering a grudge or a grievance can have the same results.

"Do a long, slow burn and you hurt no one but yourself. The man who broods over a wrong poisons his own soul.

"Repayment? Impossible! Revenge? Impotent! Resentment? Impractical!"[2]

I Don't Feel Like It!

"My mother really embarrassed me in front of my friends," Ruth said, her blue eyes flashing. "She's always doing that. I can't forgive her."

"Can't or won't?" I replied.

"I just don't feel like it!" she almost shouted.

"I just don't feel like it!" Have you ever wondered how much work would be accomplished if everyone waited until he or she felt like doing it? Have you ever really felt like washing the dishes, cleaning the garage or at least the messy drawer by the phone? When was the last time you felt like cleaning dirty diapers in the toilet?

Whenever I was sick as a child, I used to stay home from school and listen to the radio. There were great programs like "Stella Dallas," "Ma Perkins," and "The Shadow" with "Lamont Cranston and his lovely companion Margo Lane." I used to watch my father when he was sick: he still went to work. I never could understand that. Why did he go to work when he didn't feel like it? When I didn't feel like it, I stayed home from school. Then I grew up and became a man. And then I understood: my father was a responsible person.

George MacDonald pokes some fun at feelings when he writes, "They had a feeling, or a feeling had them, till another feeling came and took its place. When a feeling was there, they felt as if it would never go; when it was gone they felt as if it had never been; when it returned, they felt as if it had never gone."

Forgiveness is not a feeling first. It is a choice that goes beyond feelings; it is an activity of the will. You may respond, "If I were to forgive someone when I didn't feel like it, I would be a hypocrite." This is another great lie. If you forgive even when you don't feel like it, you are a responsible person—not a hypocrite.

For several years I conducted a men's Bible study at six o'clock in the morning. I would set two alarm clocks. When the alarms went off, what do you think my body would say? "Stay in bed." Was I a hypocrite because I went to the Bible study when my body didn't feel like it? No, I was a responsible person doing what needed to be done.

If, however, I had jumped out of bed in the morning and said, "Boy, do I love to get up at this hour!" I would have been a hypocrite! I really believe that if God wanted us to enjoy sunrises, He would have had them come at ten o'clock.

When Jesus said, "Love your enemies," He did not say have a loving feeling toward them. It would probably be a long time before you felt like loving your enemies. The apostle

Paul, quoting from the Old Testament, wrote, "If your enemy is hungry, feed him; if he is thirsty, give him something to drink" (Romans 12:20, NIV; see Proverbs 25:21). True love is basically an activity, not merely a feeling. Most people wrongly think of it as a feeling first of all.

Reviving a Marriage

When couples come to me for marriage counseling, it is not uncommon for one or both of the parties to say, "I don't feel as if I love her anymore." I never argue this point. I believe they are telling the truth; they really do feel that the love has died. Rather, I smile and ask, "Would you like to feel it again?" The usual reaction is disbelief: Is it possible for love to return? The answer is, Yes, love can be rekindled, revived, renewed.

I tell the couple that the reason their love has diminished is that they have stopped doing loving activities for each other. Never has a person seeking marital counseling said to me, "I've got to get out of this marriage, because my mate is too good to me. She loves me too much. I can't stand it anymore!" No, it is just the opposite. Love is revived by the revival of loving activities toward the other person—even if he doesn't feel like it! This is not being a hypocrite; this is being a responsible person!

I also caution the responsible person that he will probably last only three days with this attitude if he is not careful. One person will sincerely try hard, "bending over backward" or "standing on his head"—as the sayings go—to do loving activities. The other person will be a little slower in expressing this and in responding to the loving actions. It is as if she is watching something that does not seem possible or will not last. The person who is really putting himself into changing the situation will get a little discouraged after three days or so. He is not getting enough encouragement or affirmation from the other person. Finally he stops doing loving actions. Then the other person, who was holding back, says, "Aha! I knew it wouldn't last! It was just as I thought—a game. He doesn't really care."

Then the destruction starts over again in a vicious circle. I try to encourage the responsible person to continue beyond three days—beyond the fickle feelings that come and go. I encourage him to stick to a definite plan of loving activities whether or not he is loved in return. This is exactly what God does for us: He loves us and continues to love us regardless of how sinful we are. That is amazing!

Many people have trouble loving and doing loving actions because they don't feel like forgiving. Jay Adams suggests that forgiveness is not a feeling, but a promise or commitment. It is a promise or commitment to three things:

1. I will not use it against my mate in the future.
2. I will not talk to others about my mate.
3. I will not dwell on it myself.[3]

I am reminded of the man who came rushing into the marriage counselor's office and said, "You've got to help me! My wife is historical!"

"You mean hysterical!" replied the counselor.

"No, historical! She keeps bringing up the past!"

The past is brought up because it hasn't been forgiven. True forgiveness does not resurrect the past. True forgiveness is not a "vigilante" getting its victim dead or alive. Revenge is not in the heart of forgiveness. If revenge is present, forgiveness is not.

Adams suggests that:

1. God hasn't given you the authority (right) to take vengeance.
2. God hasn't given you the ability to take vengeance.
3. Nor has God given you the knowledge of what is truly fair.[4]

Mark Twain said, "Forgiveness is the fragrance the violet sheds on the heel that has crushed it." The Book of Proverbs says, "He who is slow to anger has great understanding, but he who is quick-tempered exalts folly" (Proverbs 14:29, NASB). "A man's discretion makes him slow to anger, and it is his glory to overlook a transgression" (Proverbs 19:11, NASB).

Are you exercising discretion? Are you a person who understands? Do you overlook trangressions? Romans 12:16–21 instructs us to "be of the same mind toward one another; do not be haughty in mind, but associate with the lowly. Do not be wise in your own estimation. Never pay back evil for evil to anyone. Respect what is right in the sight of all men. If possible, so far as it depends on you, be at peace with all men. Never take your own revenge, beloved, but leave room for the wrath of God, for it is written, 'Vengeance is Mine, I will repay,' says the LORD. 'But if your enemy is hungry, feed him, and if he is thirsty, give him a drink; for in so doing you will heap burning coals upon his head.' Do not be overcome by evil, but overcome evil with good" (NASB).

In an article entitled *"Christian Vigilantes?"* Jay Adams says of the above verses, "The general guiding principle that covers all Paul has written in this section is, 'Do not be overcome by evil, but overcome evil with good.' This is the battle order Christ issued to His church. You are to win your battles with evil. We have been trying to see how God expects us to do that. We've talked about many of the specific details behind those orders that appear in verses 14–18. Now we come to verse 19. This verse clarifies a perplexing aspect of the program by adding a very crucial element to it: We do not have to fight this war alone; not even together with the rest of the army. There are aspects of the war that will be handled by the Commander-in-Chief Himself.

"Had you not been told this, you might have supposed that the war depended solely upon you and others like you. You know your orders; but you often forget them. You know your orders; but you have trouble following them. And you know that others in the army are not always dependable either. Thankfully, the wise Commander has kept for Himself the ultimate issue of all things, and those aspects of the war that you and I never could have handled anyway. This is a great encouragement.

"Verse 19 reads: 'Never take your own revenge, beloved, but leave room for wrath. It is written, "Vengeance is Mine; I will repay, says the Lord." '

"We have discovered that a Christian's attitude and his actions are to be good. Good actions, based upon an understanding of the Scriptures and a desire to please God by obedience to them, will lead to good attitudes. Focusing on the person who had wronged you—his needs and problems—rather than yourself (for instance) will help avoid self-pity and will lead to a better attitude for witnessing to him and winning him. Planning ahead is another action that can have a lot to do with the attitude that one has when he finds himself engaged in hand-to-hand combat with evil on the field of battle. All this we have seen, and because we have these foundational truths fixed in mind it is possible to go on.

"Verse 19 teaches additional truth that is critical to waging war successfully. It says, in effect, that your actions and attitudes will be influenced by your understanding and acceptance of the biblical limitations placed upon your authority and ability as an individual soldier in the Lord's army. In meeting evil with good, you have a limited, circumscribed and clearly defined sphere of activity that you may not go beyond. When you do, you give aid to the enemy, usurp the authority that has been reserved for Another and endanger yourself in the bargain.

"In setting forth these limitations, the apostle used his second absolute: 'Never take your own revenge.' It is really a reiteration of the one previously given in verse 17, 'Never pay back evil for evil,' with a slightly different emphasis, to which an important reason and promise is appended: 'Vengeance is Mine, I will repay.' When Paul says never, he means just that. There is never a time when the Christian—as an individual —on his own authority may take vengeance on another. There are no special circumstances. The rule admits of no qualifications.

" 'But no one else seems to be doing anything about it; if I don't, he'll get away with what he did!' The objection is invalid. God has said He will take care of the matter in His time and His way. There are no exceptions to the rule. God's surveillance of the situation is complete; He misses nothing. There will be no failures in His justice. Your impatience in view of this verse is really impertinence! Hands off! Vengeance does not belong to you!

" 'But, I can do it so easily. I'm in a perfect position as his boss to do so. I could right all the wrongs and everyone would be happier. Perhaps, in the long run, he would be too.' No exceptions. You are never in the right position to execute justice as a private person. God has reserved that position for Himself. Step aside; you are standing where you have no right to be."[5]

**I Never Say Anything About Someone
Unless It Is Good . . . and Boy, Is This Good!**

You have probably heard about the four ministers who got together to confess their sins to each other. The first one said, "My sin is that after the morning service, my throat is so dry that I go home and have a beer." And everyone groaned and said, "That's terrible!"

The next one said, "My sin is that after the morning service, I go home and smoke a great big cigar." "Oh, that's awful!" they all moaned.

The third minister said, "My sin is that I need extra lunch money. So I take some money out of the offering." "Wow, that's wicked!" they all replied.

Finally they turned to the last man. "What is your sin?"

"I can't tell you, it's too bad."

"You've got to," they replied. "We shared ours."

"Well, if you insist. My sin is gossip, and I can hardly wait to get out of here!"

True forgiveness does not talk to others about the hurt or the offense. Relatives and friends are notorious for taking sides, especially in marital problems.

A friend of mine directs a large camping program. During one week of camp a lady came to him and related the sad story of her divorce. He asked her, "How long ago was your divorce?"

"Two years ago," she replied.

"How many people have you talked to this week about your divorce?"

"A few," she said.

"How many is a few?"

"Several," she answered.

"How many is several?" he pressed.

"Six!"

Then he said, "You know, if I were to talk to six people a week for two years about my divorce, I think I would feel like you do. I don't think that I would heal either." Forgiveness is quiet. It does not talk to others.

Jay Adams's last point about forgiveness was "I will not dwell on it myself." This is by far the hardest task . . . not to dwell on the past hurt. To dwell on past hurts over and over is like ripping your scabs to see if your cut is healing. May God help us all not to rip off the scabs of past hurts and disappointments to see if they are getting any better.

Every professional football player dreams of playing in the Super Bowl. My friend Mike Fuller was no exception. For five years No. 42 played safety for the San Diego Chargers. He also held the ball for the field-goal kicker, and he was the fourth-ranking punt-return specialist.

The Chargers looked as if they were going all the way. Even oddsmaker Jimmy the Greek picked them to win the Super Bowl. Then contract disputes sent John Jeffersen and Fred Dean to other teams, and suddenly Mike was cut from the team. Why, Lord? Mike was the inspirational force in getting the Chargers' Bible study and chapel program started. Through this program, several players came to know Christ and at least one marriage was restored.

When the Cincinnati Bengals called, he accepted . . . but not too enthusiastically. The Bengals had won six games and lost ten the previous year. No doubt Mike had some times of bitterness, but he said, "Penny and I have given ourselves to the Lord; we are His servants. Now it's time to put these things behind me and play football." So off he went to Cincinnati, where ironically his team beat the Chargers 27–7 for the league championship on the coldest day ever on which a pro football game was played. Mike played almost the entire time the Bengals' defensive unit was on the field.

Sports pages carried his comment as he left for the Super Bowl: "I'm so glad the Chargers sent me to Cincinnati!" But it didn't take that victory to make him glad. With God's help, forgiveness came easy in the season . . . or he wouldn't have made the team.

The Man About Which the Bible Says No Evil

The Old Testament relates the story of a man who is the classic example of one who forgives those who hurt him. Joseph's story is found in Genesis 37—50.

Joseph was sold into slavery by his brothers, cast into prison on a false charge, and forgotten by those he helped. If anyone had a right to be angry, it was Joseph. If anyone had reason to seek vengeance, it was Joseph. If anyone had it in his power to take revenge, it was Joseph—for he eventually became second in command to the Egyptian Pharaoh. How did Joseph respond?

More than twenty years after they sold him into slavery, Joseph's brothers came before him begging for food—not knowing who he was or what had happened to him. We read in the Bible:

"Then Joseph could not control himself before all those who stood by him, and he cried, 'Have everyone go out from me.' So there was no man with him when Joseph made himself known to his brothers. And he wept so loudly that the Egyptians heard it, and the household of Pharaoh heard of it.

"Then Joseph said to his brothers, 'I am Joseph! Is my father still alive?' But his brothers could not answer him, for they were dismayed at his presence. Then Joseph said to his brothers, 'Please come closer to me.' And they came closer. And he said, 'I am your brother Joseph, whom you sold into Egypt. And now do not be grieved or angry with yourselves, because you sold me here; for God sent me before you to preserve life. For the famine has been in the land these two years, and there are still five years in which there will be neither plowing nor harvesting. And God sent me before you to preserve for you a remnant in the earth, and to keep you alive by a great deliverance.

"'Now, therefore, it was not you who sent me here, but God; and He has made me a father to Pharaoh and lord of all his household and ruler over all the land of Egypt.' . . . And he kissed all his brothers and wept on them, and afterward his brothers talked with him" (Genesis 45:1–8, 15, NASB).

Joseph forgave his brothers without holding their crime against them, without talking to others about them, and by not dwelling on it himself. We then discover in Genesis 50:15–21: "When Joseph's brothers saw that their father was dead, they said, 'What if Joseph should bear a grudge against us and pay us back in full for all the wrong which we did to him!' So they sent a message to Joseph, saying, 'Your father charged before he died, saying, "Thus you shall say to Joseph, 'Please forgive, I beg you, the transgression of your brothers and their sin, for they did you wrong.' " And now, please forgive the transgression of the servants of the God of your father.' And Joseph wept when they spoke to him.

"Then his brothers also came and fell down before him and said, 'Behold, we are your servants.' But Joseph said to them, 'Do not be afraid, for am I in God's place? And as for you, you meant evil against me, but God meant it for good in order to bring about this present result, to preserve many people alive. So therefore, do not be afraid; I will provide for you and your little ones.' So he comforted them and spoke kindly to them" (NASB).

David Augsburger suggests that—

1. The grease of forgiving love can reduce the friction and salve the irritation.
2. Forgiveness is not holy amnesia which erases the past—instead it is the experience of healing that draws the poison out. You may recall that hurt but you will not relive the hurt.
3. The hornet of memory may fly again, but forgiveness has drawn out the sting.[6]

We read: "And so, as those who have been chosen of God, holy and beloved, put on a heart of compassion, kindness, humility, gentleness and patience: bearing with one another, and forgiving each other, whoever has a complaint against any one: just as the Lord forgave you, so also should you" (Colossians 3:12–13, NASB). Also, "Be kind to one another, tender-hearted, forgiving each other, just as God in Christ also has forgiven you" (Ephesians 4:32, NASB).

In the next chapter we will look at what is involved in helping us not to dwell on past hurts and anger. For an in-depth study of forgiveness I highly recommend two books by David Augsburger: *The Freedom of Forgiveness* and *Caring Enough to Forgive/Caring Enough Not to Forgive.*[7]

Insight Questions on Forgiveness

1. I have had trouble forgetting _____

_____

_____

_____

2. I have been having trouble forgiving the following person(s): _____

   _____

3. The situation or circumstances that have made if difficult for me to forgive are _____

   _____

   _____

   _____

4. Repayment of the offense would involve _____

   _____

   and would accomplish _____

   _____

5. Revenge would accomplish _____

   _____

6. Resentment would accomplish _____

   _____

7. With regard to the above offense(s) I ( ) Am not going to forgive them ( ) I am not yet ready to forgive ( ) I am getting closer to forgiving ( ) I will now choose to forgive them.

8. If I were to start doing loving activities to those who hurt me I would begin by _____

   _____

   _____

   then I would proceed to _____

   _____

   _____

Thoughts on Forgiveness

"Without forgiveness life is governed by an endless cycle of resentment and retaliation."   —*Roberto Assagioli*

"Nobody ever forgets where he buried the hatchet."

—*Ken Hubbard*

"Only the brave know how to forgive."

"The offender never pardons."

"To understand is to forgive."

"There is no revenge so complete as forgiveness."

—*Josh Billings*

"It is easier to forgive an enemy than a friend."

"A small boy, repeating the Lord's Prayer one evening, prayed: "And forgive us our debts as we forgive those who are dead against us.' "

"Every person should have a special cemetery lot in which to bury the faults of friends and loved ones."

"He who has not forgiven an enemy has never yet tasted one of the most sublime enjoyments of life."   —*Lavater*

"A Christian will find it cheaper to pardon than to resent. Forgiveness saves the expense of anger, the cost of hatred, the waste of spirits."   —*Hannah More*

12.

The Other Side of Forgiveness

"I am at the point where I don't even think God exists. But something deep in me says He is there. I surely don't feel like it, though. I pray and pray, but I don't seem to find any release. I don't think God hears my prayers. I still feel terrible. I know I shouldn't be this way, but I am this way!" Christy said as the tears began to flow down her face.

Christy went on, "Every religious radio program I turn on seems to say that I must learn to forgive as God forgives. Last week I talked to my minister and he said, 'Christy, you must forgive Clark!' I told him that I have tried but it doesn't seem to be working. Is there any way out? Do I have to feel this way forever?"

Christy's story is not uncommon. She has been deeply hurt. Her husband Clark had an affair with a close friend of hers. And this affair was not Clark's first; there had been three others that she knew about. Each time she forgave him and took him back. The last affair was harder on Christy than any of the others, because it involved one of her best friends. At the time Christy came to my office, Clark was still involved with the woman.

"I asked Clark if he wanted a divorce," Christy said. "He said, 'I have no intentions of getting a divorce.' I want to forgive him, I think. It is becoming harder each time. This time has been the hardest." Christy wept.

Cry Wolf

Like many others, Christy is caught in the middle of what I call "The Little-Boy-Who-Cried-Wolf Syndrome." No doubt, you recall the story of the little boy who cried "Wolf." The lad was all alone tending sheep. He thought to himself that he would like to talk with someone, but he could not leave the sheep. So he decided that if he were to yell "Wolf, Wolf!" the people in the nearby village would come out to help him protect his sheep. When they came, then he would have someone to talk to.

The boy put his plan into action several times. Just as he expected, the villagers came running to his aid. However, when they discovered that there was no wolf, they became very angry. They told him, "You had better stop crying 'Wolf' when there is no wolf, for some day when there is a real wolf, we won't come to your aid."

Then one day it happened: a real wolf attacked his sheep. The youth began to cry "Wolf, Wolf!" but no one came to his aid. All his sheep were killed. He had cried "Wolf" once too often—no one believed him anymore.

Christy was at the point where she would no longer come to Clark's aid in the form of forgiveness. He had cried "Wolf" once too often. Why was it so difficult for Christy to forgive? It was because Clark was not changing. He was not ending the affair. He was not stopping having affairs in general. He was not turning from his sin. In other words, there was no repentance in Clark's life.

Lack of repentance (change of one's lifestyle, attitude, or behavior) hinders, stifles, frustrates, and blocks the forgiveness process.

The goal of forgiveness is restoration and reconciliation of the relationship. If reconciliation does not take place, we do not have completed forgiveness . . . but frustrated forgiveness. Frustrated forgiveness is difficult to live with. Frustrated forgiveness is what Christy was living with, because there was no repentance (about-face) to Clark's sinful involvement, and hence, no reconcilation in their relationship.

This is a difficult situation to live with. But even harder is the fact that there may never be reconciliation. The relationship may never be restored. Then what is Christy supposed to do with her feelings?

In his book *Caring Enough Not to Forgive* David Augsburger deals with this point: "When forgiveness is seen primarily as an act of one-sided sacrifice, of one-way self-

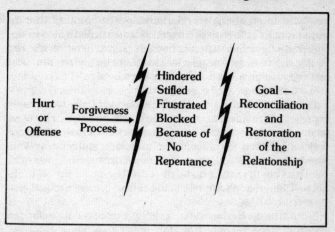

substitution, of one person absorbing the pain of another, then one-way is the way. There are times when sacrifice, acceptance, absorption are appropriate acts in forgiving, but they are the exception in times of extremity. Genuine forgiveness in ongoing relationships is not a unilateral action, but a mutual interaction. The basic model for genuine forgiveness is two-way, two-person, two movements toward reconciliation.

" 'I resented Jim for the way he worked against me at the factory. He gained nothing by undercutting me. I lost the promotion. I decided I'd never forgive him, not to my dying day. But I found I couldn't live that way. I was destroying myself with hate. It was no good, no good at all. I decided to live and let live, to forgive and forget.'

"One is a lonely number when a person is under stress or when relationships are distressed. To accept, absorb, adjust as an individual without interaction with the other party involved in the injury only increases the isolation and loneliness already involved in pain.

"One alone can change his or her attitude toward another, can plan new behaviors in response to the other, can put this into action toward the other, but until this is experienced with the other, forgiveness is frustrated.

"In the family, when one sibling must make a silent adjustment to an alienated relationship with another, the interpersonal conflict gets absorbed and turned into an intrapersonal conflict. The hurt which existed between the two is internalized by one of the two. Loneliness results. The problem has just been moved, not removed.

"In a marriage, when one partner chooses to make a private adjustment to a painful trauma between the two, it may reduce the tensions that separate them, but at a price. And as one person pays that price, loneliness increases, distance widens between them, and the marriage suffers a serious loss of openness and genuineness. Turning the pain of a relationship inward is no favor to the person or the relationship. The tensions are not being reduced, they are just getting recycled.

"In working relationships, when one person opts to forgive in quiet acquiesence, the staff spirit may show improvement, but the progress is temporary. The trust level is blocked along with the obstructed communication. The loneliness of one human privately doing the work that rightfully belongs to two, of one person needing to secretly stifle the longing for open clear communication in order to maintain a surface of cooperation, slowly separates colleagues and turns them into polite stangers. The frustration is not being dissipated, it is displaced.

"This stress on the importance of mutual forgiving flies in the face of most common understandings of what forgiveness is about. Most commonly it is taught as the one-way, one-up, one-for-all virtue. In fact, the superiority of one-way generosity, the "true spirituality" of unilateral altruism is so widely praised by preachers that real reconciliation has become the exception instead of the rule.

"Individualism as a life-style has come to be understood as the real nature of mature living, individual love-styles are seen as the norm for resolving irritations; so individual solutions have replaced the joint solutions that create real community. The goal of forgiveness is reconciliation, not release. The task of forgiving is the reconstruction of the relationship, not pious retreat from real relating. One cannot do the real work of forgiving alone. One can restore his or her perception of love as an individual step. One can respond again to the other as a precious, valued and prized person. One can initiate conversation, invite real communication and do all that is within one person's power to create a genuine trusting-risking friendship. Yet is takes two to reconcile, two to realize that we are back in right relationships again. Trying to do all this in one-way actions is a lonely way; one-way action leaves one wanting."[1]

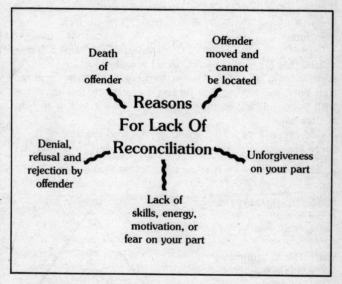

Death
of
offender

Offender
moved and
cannot
be located

**Reasons
For Lack Of
Reconciliation**

Denial,
refusal and
rejection by
offender

Unforgiveness
on your part

Lack of
skills, energy,
motivation, or
fear on your part

There is no doubt that reconciliation of the relationship must be attempted. We are instructed in Matthew 18:15–34 to do this. But what if reconciliation does not take place? What do we do then? What if the person has died? What if the person has moved away and cannot be located? What if the person denies, refuses, or rejects reconciliation?

Then forgiveness is partial. It is incomplete. It is frustrated. It is painful. It is a deep wound. And that is the way it is. Let go of it. Leave it in the Lord's hands . . . and move on.

You say, "That really hurts!" True. Now you know in a small way what God must feel to a gigantic degree. God offers forgiveness to all who have sinned against Him. He offers forgiveness to those who continue to sin against Him. But most reject, deny, and refuse to accept His forgiveness. It is one-sided. There is no acknowledgment of wrong, no repentance; God's forgiveness is frustrated and blocked and will some day end in eternal separation. That hurts Him.

How Do I Change My Emotions?

If we must let go of the hurt, how do we do it? You may say, "I keep thinking about it all the time. How do I change my emotions?"

Recently I came upon 2 Corinthians 2:1: "But I determined this for my own sake, that I would not come to you in sorrow again" (NASB). As I began to ponder the verse I realized that Paul was saying that he could determine (an act of the will) to change his emotions (sorrow). The question is, How is this done?

God created us with a mind, a will, and emotions. These three are separate, yet they interlock, overlap, and interplay with each other.

Mind: The thinking side of our being

Will: The volitional or doing side of our being

Emotions: The feeling side of our being

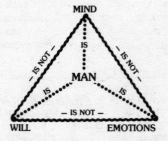

Many people live on an emotional level only. They are swayed, overpowered, and controlled by their emotions or feelings. The apostle Paul suggests that it is possible to live on a different level.

I will try to illustrate a very complicated and involved process. In the illustration that follows you will note dotted arrows leading from the emotions to the mind and the will.

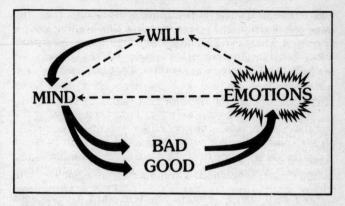

The dotted arrows indicate that the emotions do not have direct control over the mind or the will. Your emotions have only indirect control; they send out feelings and suggestions to the will and to the mind. For example, you don't "feel good" so your emotions say, "Don't go to work." Or you don't "feel good," so your emotions say, "You must not be good. Your mind is wrong in thinking otherwise."

You will also note that the mind does not have direct control over the will, but indirect control. The solid arrows indicate that the will has direct control over the mind, and the mind has direct control over the emotions.

If your mind thinks good or positive thoughts, you will have good emotions (feelings). If your mind thinks bad or negative thoughts, you will have bad emotions (feelings). We cannot think good thoughts and have bad emotions or think bad thoughts and have good emotions. Reality just doesn't work that way.

Imagine a large pink elephant with a blue ribbon around its neck. He is standing atop a freight car of a train as it rolls down the railroad track. Can you see his large ears flapping in the wind? Can you see him toss his trunk around and trumpet as the train moves along? It's a rather humorous but pleasant scene, isn't it? But now a problem arises: the train is heading for a tunnel. There is just enough room for the boxcars to make it through the opening. You can almost feel the impact (pardon the pun) of the situation.

Now, forget completely the scene of the elephant on the train. Erase it from your mind. Pause in your reading and try to do this. Do you still see him?

Now I want you to imagine a small gray kitten playing on the floor before you as you read. He is playing with a ball of yellow yarn. See him swat the ball with his front paws? Look! There goes the ball rolling under the table.

What is the value of this exercise? I want you to realize the fact that when you see the gray kitten, you no longer see the pink elephant. Or vice versa. You can't see both pictures completely at the same time. This is true of your mind. If you think good thoughts, you have good, corresponding emotions.

Now I want to make a more important point. The will does not have direct control over the emotions. The will has direct control only over the mind.

Can you think of someone who has hurt you? Someone you are having a hard time forgiving? As you do this, you may feel some negative emotions rising, even if this hurt happened long ago. The more you think about this hurt, the higher your negative feelings rise.

Have you ever said to yourself, "I shouldn't feel this way. I'll change the way I feel toward this person"? It will never work! Your will does not have direct control over your emotions. Your will has direct control only over your mind.

The only way you can change your emotional feelings is by changing what your mind thinks about. It's just like the situation between the pink elephant and the gray kitten.

What do you think makes heroes in battle? It's not the mind. The mind says, "If I go out there to rescue my friend, the odds are I'll be shot." It's not the emotions. The emotions say, "If I go out there and get shot, it will hurt and I don't like to get hurt." It's the will that motivates the hero. The will overrides both the mind and the emotions.

You could light a candle and place it on the desk in front of you. Then you could put your book down and place your right hand over the flame. The flame would begin to burn your flesh. Immediately your emotions would say, "Ouch! It hurts!" Your mind would respond, "You stupid idiot! Your hand is burning!" But your will has the power to override the influence of your mind and emotions. Your will could keep your hand there regardless of how you felt emotionally.

Have you ever felt like *not* praising the Lord? Have you ever felt like not forgiving someone? Have you been overpowered by all of your angry emotions? You can change all that if you want to. You have within your being the power to change how you feel! It comes by an exercise of your will. Your will has direct control over your mind and what it thinks about. If your want to change your emotions, the only way you can do it is by changing what your mind is thinking about.

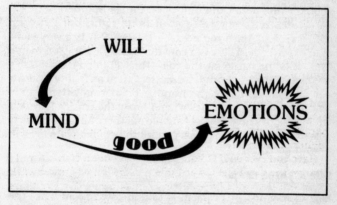

You may respond by saying, "This sounds like the Power of Positive Thinking." It is! And where do you think the positive-thinking writers got the concept? Do you know that this is a biblical idea?

Let's look at Philippians 4:4–9: "Always be full of joy in the Lord; I say it again, rejoice! Let everyone see that you are unselfish and considerate in all you do. Remember that the Lord is coming soon. Don't worry about anything; instead, pray about everything; tell God your needs and don't forget to thank him for his answers. If you do this you will experience God's peace [emotional], which is far more wonderful than the human mind can understand. His peace will keep your thoughts and hearts [mind] quiet and at rest as [an act of the will] you trust in Christ Jesus.

"And now, brothers, as I close this letter let me say this one more thing: Fix [an act of the will] your thoughts [mind] on what is true and good and right. Think [mind] about things that are pure and lovely, and dwell on the fine, good things in others. Think [mind] about all you can praise God for and be glad about. Keep putting into practice [an act of the will] all you learned from me and saw me doing, and the God of peace [emotional experience] will be with you" (LB).

To Will or Not to Will

"I know I should not live on the emotional level. I know I should think about the fine, good things in others. But it's hard to exercise my will. I want to do right, but I end up doing wrong." Have you ever felt this way? It is a very common experience. There is a constant struggle going on in our lives. It is the battle for the will—the will to do right.

Why do I neglect mundane matters such as failing to clean out the garage, doing the ironing, or writing letters to my relatives? Why do I tell lies when I know the truth? Why do I fail to seek to know God as I should? Is there an answer? Is it possible to find the necessary spark to help motivate my will toward good?

Life's Three Steps

Part of solving any problem is to understand just what the problem is. What motivates you to do anything in this life? The following chart may help you to understand human motivation.

Objective = **Goal** or purpose to be achieved

Means = **Methods** used to reach the desired objective

Effort = **Energy** required, using means to reach the end

Example A

OBJECTIVE: Reduce and lose unnecessary weight

MEANS: 1. Cut off your head and lose ten ugly pounds
                2. Stop eating

3. Metrecal
4. Ayds
5. Stillman Water Diet
6. Jack LaLanne
7. Eat smaller portions
8. Die

EFFORT: An extreme amount

Example B

OBJECTIVE: To be first string on the football team

MEANS:
1. Block
2. Tackle
3. Hurt
4. Study plays
5. Bleed

EFFORT: A great deal of it

Example C

OBJECTIVE: To be a doctor

MEANS:
1. Go to school forever
2. Be a good listener
3. Learn to write illegibly
4. Learn to carve
5. Learn to make out bills clearly

EFFORT: An exceeding amount

Everything in life revolves around the principle of Objective, Means, and Effort. We cannot reach any objective, secular or spiritual, without involving all three steps.

Can you believe that someone can lose weight without using the means and effort? What do you think the football coach would say to a young man who wants to be on the first string, but does not attend practice? Or, what of the man who walks into the hospital and wants to perform an operation but has no training and experience? Do you think the staff would let him operate? The same principle applies to the Christian life: Objective, Means, and Effort.

OBJECTIVE: To be a Spirit-filled, Spirit-led,
            joyful Christian

MEANS: 1. Receive Christ as Savior and Lord
            2. Study the Bible
            3. Pray
            4. Share your faith
            5. Fellowship with other believers
            6. Obedience to the Holy Spirit
            7. Controlling anger, forgiving others, etc.

EFFORT: A vast amount

The Ultimate Question

As we look at the principle of Objective, Means, and Effort,
other questions arise. What determines the amount of effort
expended to reach the objective? How do I get motivated?

The worth of the objective determines the amount of effort
we put forth, using the means, to reach the end. How much
is it worth to you to reduce, to play first string, to be a cheer-
leader, to be a doctor, or to be a Spirit-filled, Spirit-led, joyful
Christian? How much is it worth to you to learn how to deal
with your anger? How much is it worth to you to gain peace
by forgiving those who have sinned against you? If the objective is really worthwhile to you, you *will* put forth the effort
and use the means available to reach your goal!

As the Pendulum Swings

Many people go to extremes. One group will say, "We have to exercise our God-given will. God helps those who help themselves." Another responds, "We must deny self-will and let Christ do the work in our lives." Both extremes are dangerous. If you deny your God-given will, you become a blob of protoplasm. If you strive in self-will, you cease to be Spirit-led.

The truth of the matter is that the process is a combination of wills: God's and yours. When you become Spirit-filled and Spirit-led you don't lose your personality. God uses your personality and your temperament. God has chosen to work through human beings to accomplish His will.

God does not make breakfast in the morning. God does not change your children's dirty diapers. God does not go out and work to earn a living. In our day God does not speak directly and audibly from heaven to people. God uses men and women to accomplish His work on this planet.

When Jesus was in the garden, He said, "Not My will, but Thine, be done." Can you imagine what would have happened if Jesus had not gone to the cross? Jesus also had to exercise His human will in order to accomplish the Father's will. He said, "No man takes My life; I lay it down."

Is living a joyous, Spirit-filled, Spirit-led life worth it to you? Then you will exercise your God-given free will to put forth the effort, and use the means to reach the objective. It is at the point where you step out by faith and seek to live for Christ that God meets you and the miracle of the combination of two wills takes place in your life.

The other side of forgiveness is to change what you have been thinking about. Will dwelling on the situation change anything? Do you feel better by constantly thinking about those who have hurt you? In other words, is what you have been doing working? Give it over to God. Let go of it.

There is a story of a man who came to the doctor and said, "Doctor, every time I lift my arm it hurts." The doctor said, "Then don't lift it!" Is your arm of unforgiveness hurting? Stop lifting it. Only *you* can make that decision. Is it worth enough to you? Only when it is, will changes take place.

13.

How to Deal With Your Anger

"I have been an angry man for years. In fact, I was even angry as a child. I would rant and rave, stomp, pout, hold my breath, and throw all sorts of temper tantrums," Richard said with a strong, firm voice. "As an adult I have destroyed one relationship after another with my anger. I swear at all the idiot drivers on the road and the stupid pedestrians who think they can cross the street anywhere. I have no patience with sales people, and I don't trust those in authority. In the past I have beaten my wife and children. I just can't seem to control my temper. How do I deal with all this anger?"

The first step in learning how to deal with your anger is wanting to change. Until a person really wants to do something about the problem, little will be accomplished. The next step is to determine which of the two major divisions of dealing with anger we are talking about. We can deal with anger either *before* we have the "feelings" of anger or *after* we have them.

DEALING WITH ANGER

BEFORE I AM ANGRY   **AFTER I AM ANGRY**

I. Dealing With Anger Before I "Feel Angry"

One of the best ways to deal with anger is "preventative maintenance." If you can learn to stop anger before it gets started, you will take an important and positive step forward. To help you do this, it will be helpful to review your anger history.

ANGER HISTORY

1. In general, I would say that I am ( ) A very angry person ( ) About average as an angry person ( ) A person with very little anger

2. My friends and family would say that I am ( ) A very angry person ( ) About average as an angry person ( ) A person with very little anger

3. My score on the "Anger Inventory" in chapter 5 was _____, which listed me as _____

   _____

   _____

4. With regard to "Anger and Body Language" in chapter 3, when I am angry I usually display anger nonverbally by—

   ( ) Tone of voice (inflection, pitch). Describe what you do. _____

   _____

   _____

   ( ) Facial expressions of _____

   _____

   _____

   ( ) Body movement and gestures of _____

   _____

   _____

5. With regard to "Anger and My Health," I have seen an increase of—

   ( ) Overeating   ( ) Upset stomach
   ( ) Starvation   ( ) Nervous stomach
   ( ) Headaches   ( ) Asthma, hayfever

( ) Migraine headaches   ( ) Skin Rashes (hives,
( ) Chest pains   eczema)
( ) Twitches   ( ) Throat problems
( ) Stuttering   ( ) Bladder problems
( ) Arthritis   ( ) Low back pain
( ) Neck pains   ( ) Nausea and vomiting
( ) Runny nose   ( ) Diarrhea
( ) Constipation   ( ) Ulcers
( ) High blood pressure   ( ) Heart problems
( ) Accident proneness

6. With regard to chapter 2, several members of the "Angry Family" whom I may be related to are—

Name   Brief Description

_____   _____

                            _____

_____   _____

                            _____

_____   _____

                            _____

7. In chapter 6 "The Anatomy of Mental Problems," different lifestyles for dealing with problems were mentioned. I think the lifestyle for dealing with problems that I may have chosen is—

( ) Withdrawal or   ( ) Humor
     avoidance   ( ) In and out of relationships
( ) Rebellion   ( ) Drugs or alcohol
( ) Martyr or giver   ( ) Various forms of mental
( ) Anger   illness
( ) Other _____

_____

_____

8. In chapter 7, "Why Do I Get Angry?" a number of factors were suggested as influencing anger. The ones that influence my anger the most are—

( ) Boredom   ( ) Frustration
( ) Selfishness   ( ) Criticism
( ) Injustice   ( ) Jealousy
( ) Insecurity   ( ) Revenge
( ) Envy   ( ) Physical injury or handicap
( ) Loss of sleep   ( ) Family environment
( ) General stress   ( ) Ill health in general
( ) My mood swings   ( ) Expectations for others
( ) Past experiences   ( ) My perception and
( ) Damaged love affair   interpretation of
( ) Loss of goals   the situation
( ) Social pressure   ( ) Feelings of uselessness
( ) Humiliation or   ( ) Feelings of helplessness
 embarrassment   ( ) Loss of job
( ) Feelings of rejection ( ) Loss of a loved one
( ) Fear of failure   through death
( ) Lack of privacy   ( ) Need for space
( ) Drugs and/or alcohol ( ) Self or family protection
( ) The weather   ( ) My temperament
( ) Loss of respect   ( ) My religious background
( ) Other _____

_____

9. Most often I find myself angry toward ( ) God ( ) My children ( ) My mate ( ) Those in authority ( ) My friends ( ) Injustice ( ) My parents ( ) Myself ( ) Strangers ( ) Inanimate objects ( ) Various obstacles ( ) Other _____

_____

10. I think my basic temperament type is
( ) Sanguine ( ) Choleric ( ) Melancholy ( ) Phlegmatic

11. I think that my temperament influences my angry reactions by _____

_____

_____

12. After reviewing the questions on forgiveness in chapter 11, I think some of my anger may be focused on _____

    _____

    _____

    _____

13. The time of day that I find myself getting angry most often is ( ) Morning ( ) Afternoon ( ) Evening ( ) Late evening

14. The events that are usually happening at the time of day when I get angry are _____

    _____

    _____

15. The person or people I am most angry with is/are _____

    _____

    _____

16. In regard to "Outside Help for Anger," chapter 8, I—

    ( ) Have not received Christ as my Savior and Lord.
    ( ) Am interested in receiving Christ.
    ( ) Have received Christ as my Savior, but lately He hasn't really been Lord in my life.
    ( ) Have received Christ and I am living my life as close to the scriptures as I can.

As you review your anger history, you may decide that there are certain aspects of your life that you would like to work on. Note these areas and make them a matter of prayer. You may also feel a need to receive counsel from a wise friend, minister, or counselor about these matters. Sharing your concerns with another not only helps you to verbalize your thoughts, but it will make you somewhat accountable to another for your actions. The other person will help you to keep on the track.

How blessed is the man who does not walk
  in the counsel of the wicked,
Nor stand in the path of sinners,
Nor sit in the seat of scoffers!
But his delight is in the law of the Lord,
And in His law he meditates day and night.
And he will be like a tree firmly planted
  by streams of water,
Which yields its fruit in its season,
And its leaf does not wither;
And in whatever he does, he prospers.

Psalm 1:1-3

I will bless the LORD who has counseled me;
Indeed, my mind instructs me in the night.

Psalm 16:7

The way of a fool is right in his own eyes,
But a wise man is he who listens to counsel.

Proverbs 12:15

Without consultation, plans are frustrated,
But with many counselors they succeed.

Proverbs 15:22

Listen to counsel and accept discipline,
That you may be wise the rest of your days.

Proverbs 19:20

A plan in the heart of a man is like deep water,
But a man of understanding draws it out.

Proverbs 20:5

Prepare plans by consultation,
And make war by wise guidance.

Proverbs 20:18

For by wise guidance you will wage war,
And in abundance of counselors there is victory.

Proverbs 24:6

Oil and perfume make the heart glad,
So a man's counsel is sweet to his friend.

Proverbs 27:9, all NASB

You may find it helpful to establish a plan for reading in your
aspect of need. A good start would be with a Bible study on

anger, followed by a study on forgiveness and one on patience.

You may find that you can avoid angry outbursts by avoiding situations that trigger your anger. Agreed, it is best to resolve anger-producing situations, but this is not always possible. In that case, reduce the contact to a minimum. You need to learn to premeditate your pressure points. As the adage says it, to be forewarned is to be forearmed.

> Do not associate with a man given to anger;
> Or go with a hot-tempered man,
> Lest you learn his ways,
> And find a snare for yourself.
>
> *Proverbs 22:24–25*, NASB

You need to realize also that you are responsible to choose how you will respond in anger-producing situations. No one "makes you angry." Anger is your response to others' actions. *You* make you angry. You may find it helpful to role-play with a friend how you can respond. Or you can rehearse in your mind, before you are under pressure, your positive responses to the emotion of anger. If you are going to attend a party and you know ahead of time that someone will be there who does not like you or whom you do not care for, you can ask for God's guidance. He will help you to respond as you should, if you are willing.

It might be helpful to relax a bit. Perhaps you have been taking life a little too seriously. Perhaps the problems are not as big as you think they are. Perhaps it would be good for you to develop a sense of humor. If we sometimes take a step backward, we can see the humorous side of life and of what we think are impossible problems.

You might learn to ask yourself questions like What would Jesus do in this situation? How would He respond? Do I need to get angry? Will anger help me to handle the issue or conflict any better?

Ask God to help you to learn how to control your tongue. Someone has said, "The tongue is in a wet place and easily slips." The key for controlling your tongue is to plan ahead. Decide before you get into a stress situation that you won't speak to hurt and destroy the other person. God will give you the strength to do this if this is your desire. In James 3:2-18 we read:

> For we all stumble in many ways. If anyone does not stumble in what he says, he is a perfect man, able to bridle the whole body as well. Now if we put the bits into the horses' mouths so that they may obey us, we direct their entire body as well. Behold, the ships also, though they are so great and are driven by strong winds, are still directed by a very small rudder, wherever the inclination of the pilot desires.
>
> So also the tongue is a small part of the body, and yet it boasts of great things. Behold, how great a forest is set aflame by such a small fire! And the tongue is a fire, the very world of iniquity; the tongue is set among our members as that which defiles the entire body, and sets on fire the course of our life, and is set on fire by hell.
>
> For every species of beasts and birds, of reptiles and creatures of the sea, is tamed, and has been tamed by the human race. But no one can tame the tongue; it is a restless evil and full of deadly poison. With it we bless our Lord and Father; and with it we curse men, who have been made in the likeness of God; from the same mouth come both blessing and cursing. My brethren, these things ought not to be this way.
>
> Does a fountain send out from the same opening both fresh and bitter water? Can a fig tree, my brethren, produce olives, or a vine produce figs? Neither can salt water produce fresh. Who among you is wise and understanding? Let him show by his good behavior his deeds in the gentleness of wisdom. But if you have bitter jealousy and selfish ambition in your heart, do not be arrogant and so lie against the truth. This wisdom is not that which comes down from above, but is earthly, natural, demonic. For where jealousy and selfish ambition exist, there is disorder and every evil thing. But the wisdom from above is first pure, then peaceable, gentle, reasonable, full of mercy and good fruits, unwavering, without hypocrisy. And the seed whose fruit is righteousness is sown in peace by those who make peace (*NASB*).

Lastly, determine that you will be honest and loving whenever possible.

> Wrath is fierce and anger is a flood,
> But who can stand before jealousy?
> Better is open rebuke
> Than love that is concealed.
> Faithful are the wounds of a friend,
> But deceitful are the kisses of an enemy.
>
> *Proverbs 27:4-6*

Therefore, laying aside falsehood, speak truth, each one of you, with his neighbor, for we are members of one another.

Ephesians 4:25

Love is patient, love is kind, and is not jealous; love does not brag and is not arrogant, does not act unbecomingly; it does not seek its own, is not provoked, does not take into account a wrong suffered, does not rejoice in unrighteousness, but rejoices with the truth; bears all things, believes all things, hopes all things, endures all things. . . . But now abide faith, hope, love, these three; but the greatest of these is love.

1 Corinthians 13:4–7, 13, all NASB

It may be honest to tell your teen-age daughter that she has a big pimple on her nose . . . but it may not be the most loving thing to do.

II. Dealing With Anger After I "Feel Angry"

We have considered how to deal with anger before we feel angry. I hope that you have noted your angry history and the need we all have to make our angry feelings a matter of prayer. I have suggested the importance of counsel from the Word of God along with the wisdom of godly friends. Now I will focus on how to deal with anger after we "feel angry."

To clarify the anger process, I divide it into three major sections: the mental response to angry feelings, the verbal response, and the physical response.

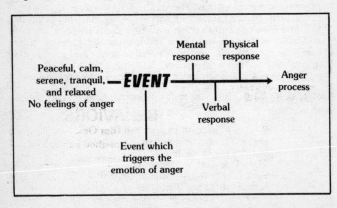

In this diagram, you will note the phrase, "Event that triggers the emotion of anger." Technically, an event in and of itself does not trigger the emotion of anger; it is actually our perception of the event that triggers the emotion of anger.

The more you perceive that someone is deliberately doing something to harm you or to irritate you, the more angry you will become. If a husband is late for dinner, the wife has a choice. She can perceive or think to herself, "I am disappointed. I went to all the work to prepare dinner and he didn't show up on time. I wish things like this wouldn't happen, but they do. I will live. I'll get over it. I'm sure he didn't do it on purpose." Or the wife can choose to say to herself, "He did that on purpose! He wants to hurt me! He wants to get revenge! He knew that I would really feel bad about this."

If the wife thinks about the situation long enough, she can build up a case against her spouse. If the wife chooses to attack her husband, he will probably respond negatively to

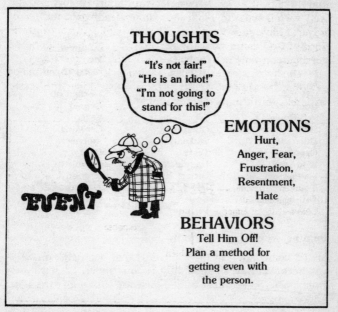

THOUGHTS

"It's not fair!"
"He is an idiot!"
"I'm not going to stand for this!"

EMOTIONS
Hurt,
Anger, Fear,
Frustration,
Resentment,
Hate

EVENT

BEHAVIORS
Tell Him Off!
Plan a method for
getting even with
the person.

her attack and say something sharp. This causes the wife to feel justified in her attack, because "You can see how he responded! He's so mean!" And round and round it goes.

An important step in dealing with anger is to face or admit your angry feelings. Recognize and admit the fact that you are angry. This is very difficult for some people to do. From childhood they were told not to be angry: "Anger is a sin. You are bad if you are angry." So they began to use other words to describe their angry feelings, because it would be terrible to admit that they were angry. Shakespeare wrote, "That which we call a rose by any other name would smell as sweet." I would like to say, "Anger by any other name is still anger."

Listed below are a few of the words we use to express that we are angry when we don't want to own up to our anger. In reality they only describe the various degrees of anger.

Begrudge	Hot	Enraged
Loathe	Repulsed	Disgusted
Disdain	Sore	Moody
Despise	Annoyed	Huffy
Abhor	Resentful	Furious
Kid	Infuriated	Inflamed
Criticize	Uptight	Mad
Scorn	Irritated	Exasperated
Laugh at	Frustrated	Irked
Grieved	Miffed	Worked up
Cool	Hurt	Griped
Fed Up	Troubled	Vexed
Sick	Offended	Crushed
Burned up	Sarcastic	Incensed
Cranky	Testy	Grumpy
Wounded	Damaged	Provoked
Catty	Bitter	Grouchy
Touchy	Mean	Ill-tempered
Out of sorts	Spiteful	Cross
Savage	Vicious	Jealous

Dealing With Anger Mentally

Listed below are a number of steps that will help you when you become aware of and admit to your anger. They will help you before you verbalize or demonstrate your angry thoughts and feelings.

1. Get more information before you respond. Sometimes

we perceive or assume that certain things are happening when they really are not. When we get more information, our thoughts and feelings may change. For example, I am sure you have heard the story about the man riding on the train with his five-year-old son. The little boy was full of energy. He bounced on the seat, he ran up and down the aisle, and he yelled a lot. A woman passenger became upset with the little boy's annoying actions. She said to herself, "Why doesn't that man teach his son some manners? He just sits there and stares out the window and is ignoring his son's misbehavior."

Finally the woman could stand the boy's actions no longer. With a firm voice she said to the father, "Sir, why don't you make your son behave! He's bothering everyone on the train!"

With a startled look, the man returned from his deep thoughts to the reality of the angry woman facing him. He said, "I . . . I'm sorry. I was deep in thought and didn't realize that he was disturbing everyone. You see, my wife died yesterday, and her coffin is in the last car. We are going back to where she was born to bury her body. I guess I just wasn't thinking about my son's actions."

When we have more information concerning an event, many times it will alter the way we feel and respond. We need to learn to ask ourselves, "Are my angry feelings justified or unjustified?"

Next time, before you lash out verbally at someone it might be good to ask a few questions first. Questions are a great way to get more information and clarify other people's words and actions. Questions like—

   a. I'm not sure that I understood what you meant. Could you please explain that a little more?
   b. I get the impression that you are upset with me. Are you?
   c. I noticed you were doing _____. Could you please help me to understand why you were doing that?
   d. I may be wrong but I feel as if there may be a problem between us. Is my perception correct?

   2. *Go to the memory file.* If you find yourself getting upset with someone, ask yourself, "Who does this person remind

me of?" If you have an overpowering, loud, and cranky boss and you feel an abnormal amount of anger, you might ask yourself whether he reminds you of your overpowering, loud, and cranky father. You may be dumping some anger felt for another onto your boss. Or you might ask yourself, "Is this situation that I'm in (and the anger I feel) similar to another situation I've been in before?" As you review your memories, you may be surprised as to how much hurt and anger you carry with you, ready to deposit it onto another person.

3. *Become aware of displaced anger.* I personally believe that 80 or 90 percent of all anger is displaced anger. By this I mean that we are angry about one thing, but we take it out on people unconnected with that. There is usually something else annoying us rather than the present event or person.

Displaced anger is exemplified by the boss who yells at his employee, who then goes home and yells at his wife, who then yells at the child. The child kicks the dog. The dog chases the cat, etc. Are you displacing your anger? Are you transfering your anger to your driving? Because of your angry thoughts, do you press harder on the gas pedal? Do you tickle your children unmercifully and not stop when they ask you to? Are you playing rougher with your dog than you should? Are you cleaning the house with quick and fast and hurried movements? Are you short of patience? Do you find yourself wishing people would hurry up and get to the point in their conversation? Then you may have a great deal of displaced anger. Ask God to help you to deal with the real cause of your anger rather than taking it out on others.

4. *Evaluate your angry feelings.* In his book *Christian Counseling*, Gary Collins encourages us to ask—

   a. What is making me feel angry?

   b. Why am I feeling anger and not some other emotion?

   c. Am I jumping to conclusions about the situation or person who is making me angry?

   d. Is my anger justified?

   e. Is it right for me to feel inferior or threatened in this anger-arousing situation?

   f. How might others, including the person who is angering me, view this situation?

g. Is there another way I could look at this situation?

h. Are there things I could do to change the situation in order to reduce my anger?[1]

5. *Remind yourself that God is in control.* God is not caught off-guard by what is happening to you. He doesn't say, "I didn't know you were going to get angry." Sometimes God allows unpleasant circumstances and events to come into our lives so that we might grow and learn to trust Him more.

> We can rejoice, too, when we run into problems and trials for we know that they are good for us—they help us learn to be patient. And patience develops strength of character in us and helps us trust God more each time we use it until finally our hope and faith are strong and steady. Then, when that happens, we are able to hold our heads high no matter what happens and know that all is well, for we know how dearly God loves us, and we feel this warm love everywhere within us because God has given us the Holy Spirit to fill our hearts with his love.   *Romans 5:3–5*

> Dear brothers, is your life full of difficulties and temptations? Then be happy, for when the way is rough, your patience has a chance to grow. So let it grow, and don't try to squirm out of your problems. For when your patience is finally in full bloom, then you will be ready for anything, strong in character, full and complete.   *James 1:2–4*

> So be truly glad! There is wonderful joy ahead, even though the going is rough for a while down here. These trials are only to test your faith, to see whether or not it is strong and pure. It is being tested as fire tests gold and purifies it—and your faith is far more precious to God than mere gold; so if your faith remains strong after being tried in the test tube of fiery trials, it will bring you much praise and glory and honor on the day of his return. You love him even though you have never seen him; though not seeing him, you trust him; and even now you are happy with the inexpressible joy that comes from heaven itself. And your further reward for trusting him will be the salvation of your souls.
> *1 Peter 1:6–9*

What a wonderful God we have—he is the Father of our Lord Jesus Christ, the source of every mercy, and the one who so wonderfully comforts and strengthens us in our hardships and trials. And why does he do this? So that when others are troubled, needing our sympathy and encouragement, we can pass on to them this same help and comfort God has given us. You can be sure that the more we undergo sufferings for Christ, the more he will shower us with his comfort and encouragement. We are in deep trouble for bringing you God's comfort and salvation. But in our trouble God had comforted us—and this, too, to help you: to show you from our personal experience how God will tenderly comfort you when you undergo these same sufferings. He will give you the strength to endure.   *2 Corinthians 1:3–7*, all LB

In *Anger: Defusing the Bomb*, Ray Burwick makes an interesting observation concerning assurance of salvation: "In nearly every severe case of a person who lacks assurance of salvation with whom I have counseled, the underlying cause has been an angry, resentful spirit. As these people worked through their bitterness, applying forgiveness, lack of assurance was no longer a problem."[2]

Are you struggling with the assurance of your salvation? Do you find it difficult to accept God's forgiveness because you have not forgiven someone in your life?

> He sat by a fire of sevenfold heat,
>   As He watched by the precious ore,
> And closer He bent with a searching gaze
>   As He heated it more and more.
> He knew He had ore that could stand the test,
>   And He wanted the finest gold
> To mould as a crown for the King to wear,
>   Set with gems with price untold.
> So He laid our gold in the burning fire,
>   'Tho' we fain would have said to Him, "Nay,"
> And He watched the dross that we had not seen,
>   And it melted and passed away.
> And the gold grew brighter and yet more bright,
>   But our eyes were so dim with tears,
> We saw but the fire—not the Master's hand,
>   And questioned it with anxious fears.
> Yet our gold shone out with a richer glow,
>   As it mirrored a Form above,
> That bent o'er the fire, tho' unseen by us,
>   With a look of ineffable love.
> Can we think that it pleases His loving heart
>   To cause us a moment's pain?
> Ah, no! But He saw through the present cross
>   The bliss of eternal gain.
> So He waited there with a watchful eye,
>   With a love that is strong and sure,
> And His gold did not suffer a bit more heat,
>   Than was needed to make it pure.
>   *Unknown*

6. Tell God how angry you are. In learning to deal with your anger you may find it helpful to read the Psalms. The psalmist often told God how angry he was. He would tell God that he needed His help. The psalmist is our example of talking to God about our anger.

I said, "I will guard my ways,
That I may not sin with my tongue;
I will guard my mouth as with a muzzle,
While the wicked are in my presence."
I was dumb and silent, I refrained even from good;
And my sorrow grew worse.
My heart was hot within me;
While I was musing the fire burned;
Then I spoke with my tongue:
"LORD, make me to know my end,
And what is the extent of my days,
Let me know how transient I am."

Psalm 39:1-4

Give ear to my prayer, O God;
And do not hide Thyself from my supplication.
Give heed to me, and answer me;
I am restless in my complaint and am surely distracted,
Because of the voice of the enemy,
Because of the pressure of the wicked;
For they bring down trouble upon me,
And in anger they bear a grudge against me.

My heart is in anguish within me,
And the terrors of death have fallen upon me.
Fear and trembling come upon me;
And horror has overwhelmed me.
And I said, "Oh, that I had wings like a dove!
I would fly away and be at rest.
"Behold, I would wander far away,
I would lodge in the wilderness.
"I would hasten to my place of refuge
From the stormy wind and tempest."

Confuse, O Lord, divide their tongues,
For I have seen violence and strife in the city.
Day and night they go around her upon her walls;
And iniquity and mischief are in her midst.
Destruction is in her midst;
Oppression and deceit do not depart from her streets.

For it is not an enemy who reproaches me,
Then I could bear it;

Nor is it one who hates me who has exalted himself against me,
Then I could hide myself from him.
But it is you, a man my equal,
My companion and my familiar friend.
We who had sweet fellowship together,
Walked in the house of God in the throng.
Let death come deceitfully upon them;
Let them go down alive to Sheol,
For evil is in their dwelling, in their midst.

As for me, I shall call upon God,
And the LORD will save me.
Evening and morning and at noon, I will complain and murmur,
And He will hear my voice.
He will redeem my soul in peace from the battle which is against
    me,
For they are many who strive with me.
God will hear and answer them—
Even the one who sits enthroned from old—Selah.
With whom there is no change,
And who do not fear God.
He has put forth his hands against those who were at peace with
    him;
He has violated his covenant.
His speech was smoother than butter,
But his heart was war;
His words were softer than oil,
Yet they were drawn swords.

Cast your burden upon the LORD, and He will sustain you;
He will never allow the righteous to be shaken.
But Thou, O God, wilt bring them down to the pit of destruction;
Men of bloodshed and deceit will not live out half their days.
But I will trust in Thee.

Psalm 55, all NASB

7. *Learn to deal with the sin of your anger.*

a. Face your anger as *sin*! The giant step in overcoming
anger is to face it squarely as sin in most cases. The minute
you try to justify it, explain it, or blame someone else, you are
incurable. I have never known anyone to have victory over a
sin unless he was convinced it was wrong! That is particularly true of anger. Consider God's commands to *Cease from
anger and forsake wrath* or *Let all bitterness and anger be
put away from you.*

b. Confess every angry thought or deed as soon as it occurs. This is giant step No. 2, based on 1 John 1:9: "If we

confess our sins, he is faithful and just to forgive us our sins and to cleanse us from all unrighteousness" (NASB).

I groaned inwardly as I read the advice a plastic surgeon offered to two men who came to him with anger-induced emotional problems. Essentially he urged them to replace their hateful thoughts by concentrating on some successful or happy experience in life. I remember asking, "But what does that do for guilt?" Absolutely nothing! The blood of Jesus Christ alone, which is adequate to cleanse us from all sin, is available to all who call upon Him in faith.

c. Ask God to take away this angry habit pattern. First John 5:14–15 assures us that if we ask anything according to the will of God, He not only hears us, but also answers our requests. Since we know it is not God's will that we be angry, we can be assured of victory if we ask Him to take away the habit pattern.

Although secular man may remain a slave to habit, the Christian must not. We are admittedly victims of habit, but we need not become addicted to patterns of conformity when we have at our disposal the power of the Spirit of God.

d. Forgive the person who has caused your anger. Ephesians 4:32 instructs us to forgive "one another, even as God for Christ's sake hath forgiven you" (KJV). If a parent, person, or "thing" in your life occupies much of your thinking, make it a special point to formally uttering a prayer of forgiveness aloud to God. Each time the hostile thoughts return, follow the same procedure. Gradually your forgiveness will become a fact, and you will turn your thoughts to positive things.

A charming illustration of this came to me after I had led a seminar for missionaries. A missionary had been plagued with anger that almost kept her from being accepted by her board. A Christian psychologist challenged her that she must forgive her father, but she replied, "I can't." He said, "You mean you won't! If you don't forgive him, your hatred will destroy you." So in his office she prayed, "Dear Heavenly Father, I do want to forgive my father. Please help me." She acknowledged having to pray that prayer several times, but finally victory came and with it the peace of God. She is a well-balanced and productive woman today because she forgave. You cannot carry a grudge toward anyone you forgive.

e. Formally give thanks for anything that "bothers" you. The will of God for all Christians is that "in every thing give thanks" (1 Thessalonians 5:18, KJV). Thanksgiving is therapeutic and helpful, particularly in reducing anger. You will not be angry or depressed if in every insult, rejection, or injury you give thanks. Admittedly this is difficult at times, but it is possible. God has promised never to burden you with anything you cannot bear (1 Corinthians 10:13). At such times, thanksgiving will have to be offered by faith, but God will even provide that necessary faith. Learn the art of praying with thanksgiving.

f. Think only good, wholesome, and positive thoughts. The human mind cannot tolerate a vacuum; it always has to dwell on something. Make sure your mind concentrates on what the Scripture approves, such as things that are "Honest, . . . just, . . . pure, . . . lovely, . . . of good report, . . . virtue, . . . and praise" (Philippians 4:8, KJV). People with such positive thoughts are not plagued by anger, hostility, or wrath. It is basically a matter of subjecting every thought to the obedience of Christ.

Anger is a habit—a temperament-induced, sinful habit —ignited through the years by distresses and unpleasant circumstances that can control a person as tenaciously as heroin or cocaine, making him react inwardly or outwardly in a selfish, sinful manner. Unless you let the power of God within you change your thinking patterns, your condition will gradually ruin your health, mind, business, family, or spiritual maturity. In addition, it grieves the Holy Spirit (Ephesians 4:30), robbing you of the abundant life that Jesus Christ wants to give you.

g. Repeat the above formula every time you are angry. Of the hundreds who claim that this simple formula has helped them, none has indicated that it happened overnight. If anger is a particular problem for you, use this formula for sixty days. Gradually God will make a new person—and you will like the new you!

Dealing With Anger Verbally

"I can't stand it any longer. I've got to talk to Frances," Connie said. "I am so angry I could spit! I haven't said a word to her. I've got to tell her how I really feel inside."

Some anger can be dealt with in our own minds, just between ourselves and God. Other anger needs to be dealt with verbally. Dealing with anger verbally is not learned overnight; it is a process.

As I have mentioned, we have to own or be responsible for our angry feelings and behaviors whether they be mental, verbal, or physical. We cannot blame others for our actions. There is a song by Anna Russell that expresses how some people refuse to take personal responsibility for their activities.

> I went to my psychiatrist
>   To be psychoanalyzed,
> To find out why I killed my cat
>   And blackened my wife's eyes.
>
> He put me on a downy couch
>   To see what he could find,
> And this is what he dredged up
>   From my subconscious mind:
>
> When I was one, my mommy hid
>   My dolly in the trunk,
> And so it follows naturally,
>   That I am always drunk.
>
> When I was two, I saw my father
>   Kiss the maid one day,
> And that is why I suffer now—
>   Kleptomania.
>
> When I was three, I suffered from
>   Ambivalence toward my brothers,
> So it follows naturally,
>   I poisoned all my lovers.
>
> I'm so glad that I have learned
>   The lesson it has taught,
> That everything I do that's wrong
>   Is someone else's fault![3]

When it comes to expressing angry feelings verbally, it will be good to remember some of the following thoughts:

1. *Learn to discipline your mind.* Think about what you're going to say before you say it. Don't just start talking, because it might be the best speech you'll ever regret. Proverbs 10:19 reads in the *New American Standard Bible,*

"When there are many words, transgression is unavoidable, but he who restrains his lips is wise." The Living Bible reads, "Don't talk so much. You keep putting your foot in your mouth. Be sensible and turn off the flow!"

2. Don't put off expressing how you feel for long periods of time. If something is bothering you and you do not share this with the person involved, you may find your angry feelings festering. Your feelings of mild irritation can grow into the poison of bitterness. "If you are angry, don't sin by nursing your grudge. Don't let the sun go down with you still angry—get over it quickly; for when you are angry you give a mighty foothold to the devil" (Ephesians 4:26–27, LB).

3. Make it a habit not to withdraw into silence. I am persuaded that 99 percent of the problems we face will not go away by themselves. They may go underground, but they don't go away. Silence does not settle any issue; it only frustrates the solution. It is usually just an excuse when we say, "I don't want to talk about it, I might hurt their feelings" or "I don't think it would do any good, they would probably just get mad." In reality, we may be afraid to talk about it. Or if we were to talk about it, we might have to forgive the person and we are not yet ready to do that.

4. Be open to criticism. No one enjoys criticism. It is painful and humbling to receive. But the truth is, we could be wrong. When you begin to talk to someone about an issue that is bothering you, you may be surprised and caught off-guard by the fact that the other person offers criticism in return. But listen to it: there may be truth in it. "It is a badge of honor to accept valid criticism" (Proverbs 25:12, LB). "If you refuse criticism you will end in poverty and disgrace, if you accept criticism you are on the road to fame" (Proverbs 13:18, LB). Someone once said, "The trouble with most of us is that we would rather be ruined by praise than saved by criticism." "Don't refuse to accept criticism; get all the help you can" (Proverbs 23:12, LB).

5. Share only one issue at a time. We usually let things build up until we are about to explode. We don't usually share how we feel at the time something happens to us. When the time comes to talk with the other party involved, we find it difficult to stick to one issue at a time. We have a tendency to back up our emotional dump truck and proceed to empty the entire load. Ask God to help you to stick to the main point or issue. Ask Him to help you to resolve conflicts one at a time.

6. *Don't use the past to manipulate other people.* It is easy to bring up past issues or past mistakes in order to make the other person feel guilty for something that is bothering you now. The past is past! Deal with the present issue. Past issues only cloud the present problem you are dealing with. Sometimes we bring up past issues only because our present argument is not strong by itself.

7. *Learn to express your expectations for others verbally.* Someone said, "If you aim at nothing, you will hit it every time." I like to say, "If you don't express verbally your expectations, how will anyone ever know what they are and how will he ever reach them for you?" The guessing game must stop! When expectations are expressed, the other person can then tell you whether he thinks he can reach them or not. You may find it helpful to write down your expectations before you share them verbally.

8. *State your hurt or complaint as objectively as possible.* Try to keep as much emotion out of the conversation as possible. Don't call the other person names as you are trying to express your disagreement. Again, you may find it helpful to write down your complaint. It may even be good to read what you have written rather than to paraphrase it.

9. *Share your complaint in private, not in public.* No one appreciates talking about personal issues when other people are around. In fact, Matthew 18:15 says, "If your brother sins, go and reprove him in private; if he listens to you, you have won your brother" (NASB). The next verse tells us what to do if he does not respond to a private talk: "But if he does not listen to you, take one or two more with you, so that by the mouth of two or three witnesses every fact may be confirmed" (18:16, NASB).

10. *Let the other party know that you are not dissatisfied with all the relationship.* Tell the other person that you are happy with other aspects of the relationship. Focus on the issue that is hindering the relationship; don't destroy the entire relationship over a single problem.

There are many moments in friendship, as in love, when silence is beyond words. The faults of our friend may be clear to us, but it is well to seem to shut our eyes to them. Friendship is usually treated by the majority of mankind as a tough and everlasting thing which will survive all manner of bad treatment. But this is an exceedingly great and foolish error; it may die in an hour of a single unwise word; its conditions of existence are that it should be dealt with delicately and tenderly, being as it is a sensitive plant and not a roadside thistle. We must not expect our friend to be above humanity.

Louise de La Ramée (Ouida)

It is harder to win back the friendship of an offended brother than to capture a fortified city. His anger shuts you out like iron bars.

Proverbs 18:19, LB

11. Avoid a win-lose situation. Are you trying to win a victory over the individual you are having difficulty with? Remember that it is possible to "win a battle and lose the war." Are you really after victory or resolution of the conflict? Sometimes we need to learn how to live with compromise. Sometimes there is not a "winning solution." What is your motivation?

12. Don't make threats to terminate or leave the relationship. Threats are usually an intimidation technique used to get the other person to conform his or her behavior to your way of thinking. Stop making idle threats; they do not help to solve anything. Determine not to run away from the relationship. This is rather like the man who was asked if he ever thought of divorce. He responded by saying, "Divorce, no! Murder, yes!" Commitment is a quality that is needed in relationships.

13. Don't always be joking. The Book of Ecclesiastes says there is "a time to laugh." But there is also a time not to laugh. Joking at a serious time divides friends; it does not bring them together. Charles H. Spurgeon said, "The joking of wits, like the playing of puppies, often ends in snarling."

14. Don't accuse or attack the other person. Learn to use "I words" rather than "you words." "I words" are assertive and confronting; "you words" are aggressive and attacking. If you really want to get into a good argument or fight, use "you words"— "You make me angry! You always do that! You never do anything right! You did that on purpose, didn't you!" "You words" make me defensive. "You words" make me want to fight. "You words" usually do not settle issues, but instead stir them up. We all need to learn how to use "I words" and own up to our own feelings. Robert E. Alberti and Michael L. Emmons suggest in their book *Your Perfect Right* that we use "I statements" such as—

"I am very angry"	"I am extremely upset"
"I am becoming very mad"	"Stop bothering me"
"I strongly disagree with you"	"I think that's unfair"
"I am very disturbed by this whole thing"	"I really don't like that"
	"Don't do that to me, please"[4]
"It bothers me"	

15. *Don't exaggerate the issue.* We sometimes exaggerate the issues in order to prove our case. It is not that we lie—we just remember big! Deal with the facts, not what we think the motivation of the other person might be. Try to look at the issue from the other person's point of view. Allow the other person to have his feelings, in the same way you have your feelings. He may be hurting also! Don't interrupt the other person when he attempts to explain his side of the issue. Listen, and don't try to prepare your case while he is talking; you will miss what he is trying to say to you.

16. *Look for a solution.* Seek reconciliation in the relationship. Is there a way to settle the issue? "Bury the hatchet" . . . but not in each other. You may find it helpful to enlist a third party who does not choose one side or the other, but will help you both to negotiate. Ask God to help you find a solution. In James 1:5–9 we read, "If you want to know what God wants you to do, ask him, and he will gladly tell you, for he is always ready to give a bountiful supply of wisdom to all who ask him; he will not resent it. But when you ask him, be sure that you really expect him to tell you, for a doubtful mind will be as unsettled as a wave of the sea that is driven and tossed by the wind; and every decision you then make will be uncertain, as you turn first this way, and then that. If you don't ask with faith, don't expect the Lord to give you any solid answer" (LB).

17. *Allow for reaction time.* If you are the initiator of a discussion, you have the advantage. There is an advantage,

because you are thinking about the issue for some time before you approach the other person. He is at a disadvantage, because he most likely has not been thinking about the issue. Give him some "think time." He needs some time to talk with God and get his own attitude right. Put yourself in his shoes. Would you like a little reaction time? I am sure you would. Extend to him the same courtesy, and he will appreciate it.

Dealing With Anger Physically

I have been asked whether it is ever right to express anger physically. I answer with a qualified yes. There may be a few times when it is not only right but necessary to express anger physically.

For example, if someone is attempting to harm your child or rape your wife or kill your husband, anger expressed physically would be appropriate. We must admit, however, that this kind of circumstance is rarely encountered.

Most physically expressed anger is potentially dangerous. It has the potential to harm, maim, or kill another person. When someone uses physical force in anger, it is usually because no other communication resources are available. He has used up all his skills or did not have them in the first place.

The person who is allowed as a child to express his anger physically may very well continue to express it that way as an adult. The major difference is that adult physical anger is harder to control than the child's. Sometimes the only way to control physical anger is with physical restraint; the most extreme form is imprisonment.

If you are struggling with physical expressions of anger now, I encourage you by all means (1) to admit your problem to yourself, (2) to admit your problem to God, and (3) to seek help from a professional counselor.

Many people are afraid, for one reason or another, to seek professional counsel. They see a stigma attached such as an implication that they are "crazy." Or they may be thinking, "I can handle it myself." The question is, Are you handling it? If you needed a plumber, you wouldn't hesitate to call one. If you needed a lawyer, you would hire one. If you were physically ill, you would go to a doctor. But when it comes to counsel for marital, family, or personal, emotional problems, the majority of people hesitate. But please do not hesitate if you are prone to physical expressions of anger. Be courageous enough to seek help with this important problem.

Appendix.

Anger in the Bible

Anger: A feeling of extreme displeasure, hostility, indignation, or exasperation toward someone or something; rage; wrath; ire.

In the New Testament, three Greek words are used to describe anger:

Orgé: A settled or abiding condition of the mind. Rises slowly. Has the view of taking revenge. Tends to be lasting in its nature. An active emotion. Ephesians 4:26a; Mark 3:5; Hebrews 3:11. Spoken against in Colossians 3:8.

Thumos (Wrath): A very agitated condition. An outburst from indignation that is within. Quick to rise up. Not so long lasting as *orgé*. Sometimes carries the idea of revenge, but not always. Quickly blazes up and quickly disappears. Ephesians 4:31.

Parogismos: A stronger form of *orgé*. Ephesians 4:26b, 6:4. Carries the idea of righteous resentment. Carries the idea "to quiver with strong emotion." Irritation and exasperation.

Counsel Regarding Anger

Leviticus 19:17-18	Thou shalt not hate thine brother in thine heart: thou shalt not in any wise rebuke thy neighbour, and not suffer sin upon him. Thou shalt not avenge, not bear any grudge against the children of thy people, but thou shalt love thy neighbour as thyself: I am the LORD.
Nehemiah 9:17c	But thou are a God ready to pardon, gracious and merciful, slow to anger, and of great kindness, and forsookest them not.

Psalm 7:11	God judgeth the righteous, and God is angry with the wicked every day.
Psalm 37:8	Cease from anger, and forsake wrath: fret not thyself in any wise to do evil.
Proverbs 11:4	Riches profit not in the day of wrath: but righteousness delivereth from death.
Proverbs 14:17, 29	He that is soon angry dealeth foolishly: and a man of wicked devices is hated. . . . He that is slow to wrath is of great understanding: but he that is hasty of spirit exalteth folly.
Proverbs 15:1, 18	A soft answer turneth away wrath: but grievous words stir up anger. . . . A wrathful man stirreth up strife: but he that is slow to anger appeaseth strife.
Proverbs 16:14, 32	The wrath of a king is as messengers of death: but a wise man will pacify it. . . . He that is slow to anger is better than the mighty; and he that ruleth his spirit than he that taketh a city.
Proverbs 17:14	The beginning of strife is as when one letteth out water: therefore leave off contention, before it be meddled with.
Proverbs 19:11, 19	The discretion of a man deferreth his anger; and it is his glory to pass over a transgression. . . . A man of great wrath shall suffer punishment: for if thou deliver him, yet thou must do it again.
Proverbs 22:24	Make no friendship with an angry man; and with a furious man thou shalt not go.
Proverbs 29:22	An angry man stirreth up strife, and a furious man aboundeth in transgression.
Jeremiah 10:24	O Lord, correct me, but with judgment; not in thine anger, lest thou bring me to nothing.
Nahum 1:3a	The Lord is slow to anger, and great in power, and will not at all acquit the wicked.
Matthew 5:22	But I say unto you, That whosoever is angry with his brother without a cause shall be in danger of the judgment: and whosoever shall say to his brother, Raca, shall be in danger of the council: but whosoever shall say, Thou fool, shall be in danger of hell fire.

Matthew 18:15-20   Moreover if thy brother shall trespass against thee, go and tell him his fault between thee and him alone: if he shall hear thee, thou hast gained thy brother. But if he will not hear thee, then take with thee one or two more, that in the mouth of two or three witnesses every word may be established. And if he shall neglect to hear them, tell it unto the church: but if he neglect to hear the church, let him be unto thee as an heathen man and a publican.

Verily I say unto you, Whatsoever ye shall bind on earth shall be bound in heaven; and whatsoever ye shall loose on earth shall be loosed in heaven. Again I say unto you, That if two of you shall agree on earth as touching any thing that they shall ask, it shall be done for them of my Father which is in heaven. For where two or three are gathered together in my name, there am I in the midst of them.

Mark 3:5   And when he had looked round about them with anger, being grieved for the hardness of their hearts, he saith unto the man, Stretch forth thine hand. And he stretched it out: and his hand was restored whole as the other.

Mark 11:15   And they come to Jerusalem: and Jesus went into the temple, and began to cast out them that sold and bought in the temple, and overthrew the tables of the moneychangers, and the seats of them that sold doves.

Acts 17:16   Now while Paul waited for them at Athens, his spirit was stirred in him, when he saw the city wholly given to idolatry.

Romans 1:18   For the wrath of God is revealed from heaven against all ungodliness and unrighteousness of men, who hold the truth in unrighteousness.

Galatians 5:20   Idolatry, witchcraft, hatred, variance, emulations, wrath, strife, seditions, heresies.

Ephesians 2:3   Among whom also we all had our conversation in times past in the lusts of our flesh, fulfilling the desires of the flesh and of the mind; and were by nature the children of wrath, even as others.

Ephesians 4:26, 31   Be ye angry, and sin not: let not the sun go down upon your wrath: ... Let all bitterness, and wrath, and anger, and clamour, and evil speaking, be put away from you, with all malice.

Ephesians 5:6   Let no man deceive you with vain words: for because of these things cometh the wrath of God upon the children of disobedience.

Ephesians 6:4   And, ye fathers, provoke not your children to wrath: but bring them up in the nurture and admonition of the Lord.

Colossians 3:8   But now ye also put off all these; anger, wrath, malice, blasphemy, filthy communication out of your mouth.

1 Timothy 2:8   I will therefore that men pray every where, lifting up holy hands, without wrath and doubting.

James 1:19-20   Wherefore, my beloved brethren, let every man be swift to hear, slow to speak, slow to wrath: for the wrath of man worketh not the righteousness of God.

A Concordance for Anger

Anger Forbidden

Ecclesiastes 7:9
Matthew 5:22
Romans 12:19

Anger a Work of the Flesh

Galatians 5:20

Anger a Characteristic of Fools

Proverbs 12:16; 14:29; 27:3
Ecclesiastes 7:9

Anger and Pride

Proverbs 21:24

Anger and Cruelty

Genesis 49:7
Proverbs 27:3-4

Anger and Strife

Proverbs 21:19; 29:22; 30:33

Anger Brings Its Own Punishment

Job 5:2
Proverbs 19:19; 25:28

Anger Comes From Grievous Words

Judges 12:4
2 Samuel 19:43
Proverbs 15:1

Anger Leads to Sin

Psalm 37:8
Ephesians 4:26

Anger Should Not Hinder Prayer

1 Timothy 2:8

Anger Can Be Stopped by Wisdom

Proverbs 29:8

Anger Is Slowed by Meekness

Proverbs 15:1

Anger Should Not Come Fast

Proverbs 15:18; 16:32; 19:11
Titus 1:7
James 1:19

Anger Should Be Avoided

Genesis 49:6
Proverbs 22:24

Anger Is Sometimes Justifiable

In Christ: Mark 3:5
Jacob: Genesis 31:36
Moses: Exodus 11:8; 32:19
        Leviticus 10:16
        Numbers 16:15
Nehemiah: Nehemiah 5:6; 13:17, 25

Anger Is Sinful Most of the Time

Cain: Genesis 4:3-8
Esau: Genesis 27:41-45
Joseph's brothers: Genesis 37:4-20
Simeon and Levi: Genesis 49:5-7
Moses: Numbers 20:10-11
Balaam: Numbers 22:27
Saul: 1 Samuel 18:8—31:4

Ahab: 1 Kings 21:4; 22:8–27
Naaman: 2 Kings 5:9–15
Asa: 2 Chronicles 16:7–13
Uzziah: 2 Chronicles 26:19
Haman: Esther 3:5—7:10
Nebuchadnezzar: Daniel 3:13; 19–26
Jonah: Jonah 4:4
Herod: Matthew 2:16
Herodias: Mark 6:18–26
Jews: Luke 4:28
Enemies of Christ: Luke 6:11
High priest: Acts 5:17; 7:54

Arrogant: Overly convinced of one's own importance; overbearingly proud; haughty; insolent; swelled up; stiff.

1 Samuel 2:3
Proverbs 8:13
Isaiah 13:11
Jeremiah 48:29

Bitterness: Strong animosity, marked by anguished resentfulness or rancor.

Bitter: To be grieved, to be squeezed or pressed down.

Embitter: To trickle, like the drops of water from the Chinese water torture; to prick with a sharp pointed object.

Deuteronomy 32:32
Proverbs 14:10
Isaiah 38:15
Jeremiah 4:18
Acts 8:23
Romans 3:14
Ephesians 4:31
Hebrews 12:15
James 3:14

Clamor: To cry out like the cry of a raven. It signifies the tumult of controversy, a vehement expression of discontent or protest.

Acts 23:9
Ephesians 4:31

Contention: Strife, quarrel, rivalry, wrangling, sharpening of the feeling, incitement, fighting, combat, factiousness, discord, striving to win.

Proverbs 13:10; 17:14; 18:6, 18–19; 19:3; 21:19; 22:10; 23:29; 26:21; 27:15
Romans 2:8
1 Corinthians 1:11, 16
Titus 3:9

Deceit: To cheat, beguile, give a false impression.

Deception: Unscrupulous words and deeds designed to deceive, a snare.

Deceive: To lead into error, to seduce.

Deceit is to be avoided: Job 31:5
Shun those who are addicted to deceit: Psalm 101:7
Pray for deliverance from deceit: Psalm 43:1; 72:14; 120:2
Beware those who teach deceit: Ephesians 5:6; Colossians 2:8
Ministers are to lay aside deceit: 2 Corinthians 4:2; 1 Thessalonians 2:3
Deceit hinders knowledge of God: Jeremiah 8:5; 9:6
Deceit leads to pride: Jeremiah 5:27–28
Deceit leads to lying: Proverbs 14:25
Hatred is concealed by deceit: Proverbs 26:24–26; 27:2
The blessedness of being free from deceit: Psalms 24:4–5; 32:2

Envy: Strong feeling of displeasure produced by witnessing or hearing or the advantage or prosperity of others; to want or strongly desire what others have.

Psalm 37:1, 7
Proverbs 3:31; 14:30; 23:17; 24:1; 27:4
Song of Songs 8:6
Romans 13:13
1 Corinthians 3:3; 13:4
2 Corinthians 12:20
Galatians 5:19–21, 26
1 Timothy 6:4–5
James 3:14, 16
1 Peter 2:1

Hatred: Malicious and unjustifiable feelings toward others, animosity, violent dislike, abhorrence.

Leviticus 19:17
Proverbs 10:12, 18; 15:17; 26:24–26
Matthew 5:43–44; 6:15
Galatians 5:19–20
Ephesians 4:31
Colossians 3:8
1 John 2:9, 11; 3:10, 13–15; 4:20

Malice: Badness in quality, viciousness in character, desire to harm others or to see others suffer, ill will, spite.

Psalm 140:1–4
Proverbs 6:14–15, 18–19; 10:6, 12; 11:17; 12:10; 14:17, 22; 15:17; 16:30; 17:5; 24:8, 17–18, 29; 28:10
Isaiah 32:6
Romans 1:28–32
1 Corinthians 14:20
Galatians 5:19–21
Ephesians 4:31
Colossians 3:8
1 Thessalonians 5:15
Titus 3:3
James 1:21
1 Peter 2:1; 3:9

Examples of Malice:

Cain toward Abel: Genesis 4:8
Ishmael toward Sarah: Genesis 21:9
Sarah toward Hagar: Genesis 21:10
Philistines toward Isaac: Genesis 26
Esau toward Jacob: Genesis 27:41
Brothers toward Joseph: Genesis 37; 42:21
Potiphar's wife toward Joseph: Genesis 39:14–20
Ammonites toward the Israelites: Deuteronomy 23:3–4
Saul toward David: 1 Samuel 18:8–29; 19; 20:30–33; 22:6–18; 23:7–23
David toward Michal: 2 Samuel 6:21–23
Shimei toward David: 2 Samuel 16:5–8
Ahithophel toward David: 2 Samuel 17:1–3
Jezebel toward Elijah: 1 Kings 19:1–2
Ahaziah toward Elijah: 2 Kings 1
Jehoram toward Elisha: 2 Kings 6:31
Samaritans toward the Jews: Ezra 4; Nehemiah 2:10; 4; 6
Haman toward Mordecai: Esther 3:5–15; 5:9–14
Nebuchadrezzar toward Zedekiah: Jeremiah 52:10
Daniel's enemies: Daniel 6:4–9
Herodias toward John: Matthew 14:3–10; Mark 6:24–28
Jews toward Jesus: Matthew 27:18; Mark 12:12; 15:10; Luke 11:53–54
James and John toward Samaritans: Luke 9:54
Jews toward Paul: Acts 17:5; 23:12; 25:3

Strife: Heated, often violent dissension, bitter conflict, a struggle between rivals.

Proverbs 6:12–14, 16–19; 10:12; 15:18; 16:28; 17:1, 14, 19; 18:6; 19:13; 20:3; 21:19; 25:8; 26:17, 20–21; 27:15; 28:25; 29:22

Romans 12:18; 13:13
1 Corinthians 1:10–13; 3:1, 3–4; 11:16–19
2 Corinthians 12:20
Galatians 5:10, 15, 19–21
Philippians 2:3, 14–15
1 Timothy 1:5–7; 2:8; 3:2–3; 6:3–5, 20–21
2 Timothy 2:14, 23–25
Titus 3:1–3, 9
James 3:14–16; 4:1–2

Patience and Forgiveness in the Bible

Patience: The capacity of calm endurance, tolerant understanding, forbearance, tolerance of something or someone over a period of time, generally without complaint though not necessarily without annoyance.

Psalm 37:7–9
Proverbs 15:18
Ecclesiastes 7:8–9
Lamentations 3:26–27
Luke 8:15; 21:19
Romans 2:7; 8:25; 12:12; 15:4–5
1 Corinthians 13:4–5
2 Corinthians 6:4–6; 12:12
Galatians 6:9
Ephesians 4:1–2
Colossians 1:10–11; 3:12–13
1 Thessalonians 1:3; 5:14
2 Thessalonians 3:5
1 Timothy 3:2; 6:11
2 Timothy 2:24–25
Titus 2:1–2, 9
Hebrews 6:12, 15; 10:36; 12:1
James 1:3–4, 19; 5:7–8
1 Peter 2:19–23
2 Peter 1:5–6
Revelation 1:9; 13:10; 14:12

Examples of Patience

Isaac; Genesis 26:15–22
Moses: Exodus 16:7–8
Job: Job 1:21; James 5:11
David: Psalm 40:1
Simeon: Luke 2:25
Paul: 2 Timothy 3:10
Prophets: James 5:10
The Thessalonians: 2 Thessalonians 1:4

The churches at Ephesus and Thyatira: Revelation 2:2–3; 2:19
John: Revelation 1:9

Forgive: To excuse for a fault or offense, to pardon, to renounce anger or resentment against, to absolve from payment of, to pass over a mistake or fault without demanding punishment or redress.

Exodus 23:4–5
Proverbs 19:11; 24:17, 29; 25:21–22
Ecclesiastes 7:21
Matthew 5:7, 39–41, 43–46; 6:12, 14–15; 18:21–35
Mark 11:25
Luke 6:35–37; 17:3–4
Romans 12:14, 17, 19, 21
1 Corinthians 4:12–13
Ephesians 4:32
Colossians 3:13
Philemon 10, 18
1 Peter 3:9

Examples of Forgiveness

Esau: Genesis 33:4, 11
Joseph: Genesis 45:5–15; 50:19–21
Moses: Numbers 12:1–13
David: 1 Samuel 24:10–12; 26:9, 23
　　　　2 Samuel 1:14–17
Solomon: 1 Kings 1:53
The prophet of Judah: 1 Kings 13:3–6
Jesus: Luke 23:34

Is it possible to experience joy, peace and happiness and to have a

Dynamic living is only found in a personal relationship with God . . . made possible by Jesus Christ.

"Jesus told him, I am the Way—yes, and the Truth and the Life. No one can get to the Father except by means of me" John 14:6.

"I came that they might have life, and might have it more abundantly" John 10:10.

To understand this concept, let's take a look at man's beginning in the Garden of Eden.

God created man in his own image. Genesis 1:27

The image of God refers to Man's mind, will and emotions.

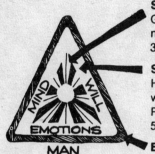

SPIRIT
God consciousness or awareness, Proverbs 20:27; Job 32:8; Psalm 18:28

SOUL
Heart of man . . . Man's mind, will, emotions. Genesis 2:7; Psalm 13:2; 1 Thessalonians 5:23; Hebrews 4:12

BODY
Physical body . . . the five senses. Genesis 1:26.

In the beginning God and man had perfect fellowship (Relationship)

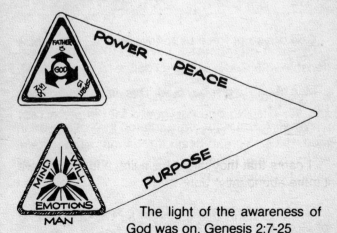

The light of the awareness of God was on. Genesis 2:7-25

Man disobeyed and his relationship with God was broken. Genesis 2:17; 3:1-24.

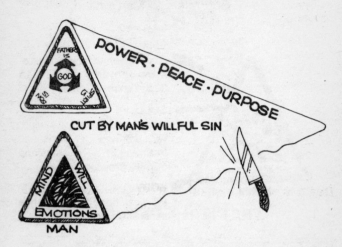

The spirit of man died toward God . . . the light was put out. Ephesians 4:18

God does not force us to love Him . . . the choice is ours.

Man chose to disobey God. This disobedience was sin.

"When Adam sinned, sin entered the entire human race. His sin spread death throughout all the world, so everything began to grow old and die, for all sinned" Romans 5:12.

"For all have sinned and come short of the glory of God" Romans 3:23.

THE WAGE OF SIN IS

Death is eternal separation from God. Romans 6:23

WHAT IS THE REMEDY?

Jesus is the only way back to God. John 14:6

Jesus restores the relationship. Romans 5:8; 1 Peter 3:18; 1 Timothy 2:5; Hebrews 9:15

How do we apply God's remedy?

RECEIVE
JESUS
INTO YOUR
HEART
BY FAITH

FREE GIFT—
Romans 6:23,
Ephesians 2:8-9

"But to all who received him, he gave the right to become children of God. All they needed to do was to trust him to save them" John 1:12, *TLB*.

What happens when one receives Jesus into his life?

GOD BY HIS
HOLY SPIRIT
ENTERS
OUR LIFE

God again turns on the light of God consciousness or awareness in the spirit of man. See Titus 3:5,6.

Would you like to experience a dynamic life? Would you like to receive Jesus?

You can by a simple prayer of faith. Remember that becoming a Christian is not just saying words . . . it's receiving a person—Jesus.

DEAR LORD JESUS,
I WOULD LIKE TO RECEIVE YOU INTO MY LIFE. THANK YOU FOR DYING IN MY PLACE. THANK YOU FOR PARDONING MY SINS. THANK YOU FOR THE GIFT OF ETERNAL LIFE. HELP ME, BY YOUR HOLY SPIRIT, TO LIVE FOR YOU.
AMEN.

"When someone becomes a Christian, he becomes a brand new person inside. He is not the same anymore. A new life has begun" 2 Corinthians 5:17.

To help you in this dynamic life . . . Jesus must be the controller of your life.

Jesus wants to reinvade your mind, will and emotions and establish his control.

Notes

Chapter 2: Meet the Angry Family

[1]The Angry Family and their relatives are stimulated by and adapted from the books *Cherishable: Love and Marriage* by David Augsburger (Scottdale, Pa.: Herald Press, 1971); *Understanding Anger in the Church* by Daniel G. Bagby (Nashville: Broadman, 1979); *How to Get Angry Without Feeling Guilty* by Adelaide Bry (New York: Signet, 1976); and *The Angry Book* by Theodore I. Rubin (New York: Macmillan, 1969).

Chapter 3: Anger and Body Language

[1]Desmond Morris et al., *Gestures: Their Origins and Distribution* (New York: Stein & Day, 1979), pp. 27–28.

[2]Gerard I. Nierenberg and Henry H. Calero, *How to Read a Person Like a Book* (New York: Pocket Books, 1971), pp. 54–56.

[3]James C. Hefley, *Searchlight on Bible Words* (Grand Rapids: Zondervan, 1972), p. 121.

Chapter 4: Anger and Your Health

[1]S. I. McMillen, *None of These Diseases* (Westwood, N.J.: Spire Books, 1973), p. 72.

[2]Ibid., p. 69.

[3]Hefley, *Searchlight on Bible Words*, pp. 119–20.

[4]Leo Madow, *Anger* (New York: Charles Scribner's Sons, 1972), p. 85.

[5]H. Norman Wright, *An Answer to Anger and Frustration* (Irvine, Calif.: Harvest House, 1977), p. 31.

[6]W. J. Grace and D. T. Graham, *Relationship of Specific Attitudes and Emotions to Certain Bodily Diseases* (Psychosomatic Classics, 1972), pp. 243–52.

[7]Dwight L. Carlson, *Overcoming Hurts and Anger* (Eugene, Ore.: Harvest House, 1981), p. 27.

[8]Theodore I. Rubin, *The Angry Book* (New York: Collier Books, 1969), pp. 54–56.

[9]Madow, *Anger*, pp. 10–11.

[10]Meyer Friedman and Ray H. Rosenman, *Type A Behavior and Your Heart* (New York: Fawcett Crest, 1974), p. 14.

[11]Ibid., p. 95.

[12]Ibid., p. 201.

[13]Ibid., p. 202.

Chapter 5: Anger Inventory

[1]David D. Burns, *Feeling Good: The New Mood Therapy* (New York: William Morrow, 1980), pp. 137–40.

Chapter 6: The Anatomy of Mental Problems

[1]Tim LaHaye, *How to Win Over Depression* (Grand Rapids: Zondervan, 1974), p. 88.

[2]Ibid., p. 89.

[3]Ibid., pp. 89–90.

[4]Louis P. Thorpe, Barney Katz, and Robert T. Lewis, *The Psychology of Abnormal Behavior* (New York: Ronald Press, 1961), pp. 122–28.

[5]Gerald D. Erickson and Terrence P. Hogan, *Family Therapy: An Introduction to Theory and Technique* (Monterey, Calif.: Brooks/Cole, 1972), p. 184.

Chapter 7: Why Do I Get Angry?

[1]Ernst G. Beier and Evans G. Valens, *People-Reading* (New York: Warner Books, 1975), pp. 68–69.

Chapter 9: Anger and Your Temperament

[1]Tim LaHaye, *Spirit-Controlled Temperament* (Wheaton, Ill.: Tyndale House, 1966); *Transformed Temperaments* (Wheaton, Ill.: Tyndale House, 1979); *Understanding the Male Temperament* (Old Tappan, N.J.: Fleming H. Revell, 1977); and Beverly LaHaye, *How to Develop Your Child's Temperament* (Irvine, Calif.: Harvest House, 1977).

Chapter 10: Is It Ever Right to Be Angry?

[1]Archibald D. Hart, *Feeling Free* (Old Tappan, N.J.: Fleming H. Revell, 1979), pp. 73–74.

[2]Elizabeth R. Skoglund, *To Anger, With Love* (New York: Harper & Row, 1977), pp. 27–29.

[3]Charles R. Swindoll, *Three Steps Forward, Two Steps Back* (Nashville: Thomas Nelson, 1980), p. 152.

Chapter 11: Anger and Forgiveness

[1]David W. Augsburger, *The Freedom of Forgiveness* (Chicago: Moody Press, 1970), pp. 20–21.

[2]Ibid., pp. 13–14.

[3]Jay E. Adams, *The Christian Counselor's Manual* (Nutley, N.J.: Presbyterian and Reformed, 1973), pp. 64–70.

[4]Jay E. Adams, *How to Overcome Evil* (Grand Rapids: Baker, 1977), pp. 89–90.

[5]Ibid., pp. 87–89.

[6]Augsburger, *The Freedom of Forgiveness*, pp. 38–39.

[7]David W. Augsburger, *Caring Enough to Forgive/Caring Enough Not to Forgive* (Scottdale, Pa.: Herald, 1981).

Chapter 12: The Other Side of Forgiveness

[1]David W. Augsburger, *Caring Enough Not to Forgive* (Glendale, Calif.: Regal Books, 1981), pp. 28–31.

Chapter 13: How to Deal With Your Anger

[1]Gary R. Collins, *Christian Counseling: A Comprehensive Guide* (Waco: Word Books, 1980), p. 109.

[2]Ray Burwick, *Anger: Defusing the Bomb* (Wheaton, Ill.: Tyndale House, 1981), p. 87.

[3]James D. Mallory, *The Kink and I* (Wheaton, Ill.: Victor Books, 1965), p. 210.

[4]Robert E. Alberti and Michael L. Emmons, *Your Perfect Right* (San Luis Obispo, Calif.: Impact Publishers, 1970), p. 84.

Bibliography

Adams, Jay E. *The Christian Counselor's Manual.* Nutley, N.J.: Presbyterian and Reformed Publishing Co., 1973.

_____. *How to Overcome Evil.* Grand Rapids: Baker Book House, 1977.

_____. *More Than Redemption.* Grand Rapids: Baker Book House, 1979.

_____. *Update on Christian Counseling.* Grand Rapids: Baker Book House, 1979.

Adler, Alfred. *Understanding Human Nature.* New York: Fawcett Premier, 1927.

Ahlem, Lloyd H. *How to Cope With Conflict, Crisis and Change.* Glendale, Calif.: Regal Books, 1978.

Alberti, Robert E., and Emmons, Michael L. *Your Perfect Right.* San Luis Obispo, Calif.: Impact Publishers, 1970.

_____. *Stand Up, Speak Out, Talk Back!* New York: Simon & Schuster, Pocket Books, 1970.

The American Heritage Dictionary. Boston: Houghton Mifflin Company, 1969.

Augsburger, David W. *Anger and Assertiveness in Pastoral Care.* Philadelphia: Fortress Press, 1979.

_____. *Caring Enough to Confront.* Glendale, Calif.: Regal Books, 1974.

_____. *Caring Enough to Forgive.* Glendale, Calif.: Regal Books, 1981.

_____. *Cherishable: Love and Marriage.* Scottdale, Pa.: Herald Press, 1971.

_____. *The Freedom of Forgiveness 70X7.* Chicago: Moody Press, 1970.

Bach, George R. *The Intimate Enemy: How to Fight Fair in Love and Marriage.* New York: Avon Books, 1968.

Bagby, Daniel G. *Understanding Anger in the Church.* Nashville: Broadman Press, 1979.

Barrett, Roger. *Depression.* Elgin, Ill.: David C. Cook Publishing Co., 1977.

Beier, Ernst G., and Valens, Evans G. *People-Reading.* New York: Warner Books, 1975.

Brandt, Henry R. *The Struggle for Peace.* Wheaton, Ill.: Scripture Press Publications, 1965.

Bresler, David E. *Free Yourself From Pain.* New York: Simon & Schuster, 1979.

Bry, Adelaide. *How to Get Angry Without Feeling Guilty.* New York: Signet Books, 1976.

Burns, David D. *Feeling Good: The New Mood Therapy.* New York: Willam Morrow & Co., 1980.

Burwick, Ray. *Anger: Defusing the Bomb.* Wheaton, Ill.: Tyndale House Publishers, 1981.

Cammer, Leonard. *Freedom From Compulsion.* New York: Simon & Schuster, 1976.

_____. *Up From Depression.* New York: Simon & Schuster, Pocket Books, 1969.

Carlson, Dwight L. *Overcoming Hurts and Anger.* Eugene, Ore.: Harvest House Publishers, 1981.

Clinebell, Howard. *Growth Counseling.* Nashville: Abingdon, 1979.

Collins, Gary R. *A Psychologist Looks at Life.* Wheaton, Ill.: Key Publishers, 1971.

_____. *Christian Counseling: A Comprehensive Guide.* Waco: Word Books, 1980.

_____. *How to Be a People Helper.* Santa Ana: Vision House Publishers, 1976.

Dobson, James. *Emotions: Can You Trust Them?* Ventura, Calif.: Regal Books, 1980.

Drakeford, John W. *Games Husbands and Wives Play.* Nashville: Broadman Press, 1970.

Dreikurs, Rudolf. *Fundamentals of Adlerian Psychology.* Chicago: Alfred Adler Institute, 1953.

Duffy, William, *Sugar Blues.* New York: Warner Books, 1975.

Ellis, Albert, and Harper, Robert A. *A Guide to Rational Living.* North Hollywood, Calif.: Wilshire Book Company, 1961.

Erickson, Gerald D., and Hogan, Terrence P. *Family Therapy: An Introduction to Theory and Technique.* Monterey, Calif.: Brooks/Cole Publishing, 1972.

Fast, Julius. *Body Language.* New York: Simon & Schuster, Pocket Books, 1970.

Faul, John, and Augsburger, David. *Beyond Assertiveness.* Waco: Calibre Books, 1980.

Ferguson, Ben. *God, I've Got a Problem.* Santa Ana: Vision House Publishers, 1974.

Filley, Alan C. *Interpersonal Conflict Resolution.* Glenview, Ill.: Scott, Foresman & Company, 1975.

Flynn, Leslie B. *Great Church Fights.* Wheaton, Ill.: Victor Books, 1976.

Friedman, Meyer, and Rosenman, Ray H. *Type A Behavior and Your Heart.* New York: Fawcett Crest, 1974.

Gaylin, Willard. *Feelings: Our Vital Signs.* New York: Harper & Row, 1979.

Glasser, William. *Mental Health or Mental Illness?* New York: Harper & Row, 1970.

_____. *Stations of the Mind.* New York: Harper & Row, 1981.

Goodstein, Leonard D., and Lanyon, Richard I. *Adjustment, Behavior, and Personality.* Reading, Mass.: Addison-Wesley Publishing, 1979.

Grace, W.J., and Graham, D.T. *Relationship of Specific Attitudes and Emotions to Certain Bodily Diseases.* Psychosomatic Classics, 1972.

Haggai, John Edmund. *How to Win Over Worry.* Grand Rapids: Zondervan Publishing House, 1959.

Hart, Archibald D. *Feeling Free.* Old Tappan, N.J.: Fleming H. Revell Company, 1979.

Hefley, James C. *Searchlight on Bible Words.* Grand Rapids: Zondervan Publishing House, 1972.

Jacobs, Joan. *Feelings! Where They Come From and How to Handle Them.* Wheaton, Ill.: Tyndale House Publishers, 1976.

LaHaye, Tim. *The Battle for the Mind.* Old Tappan, N.J.: Fleming H. Revell Company, 1980.

_____. *How to Win Over Depression.* Grand Rapids: Zondervan Publishing House, 1974.

_____. *Spirit-Controlled Temperament.* Wheaton, Ill.: Tyndale House Publishers, 1970.

_____. *Transformed Temperaments.* Wheaton, Ill.: Tyndale House Publishers, 1979.

_____. *Understanding the Male Temperament.* Old Tappan, N.J.: Fleming H. Revell Company, 1977.

Layden, Milton, *Escaping the Hostility Trap.* Englewood Cliffs, N.J.: Prentice-Hall, 1977.

Laiken, Deidre S., and Schneider, Alan J. *Listen to Me, I'm Angry.* New York: Lothrop, Lee & Shepard, 1980.

The Living Bible. Wheaton, Ill.: Tyndale House Publishers, 1971.

Lutzer, Erwin. *Managing Your Emotions.* Chappaqua, N.Y.: Christian Herald Books, 1981.

Madow, Leo. *Anger: How to Recognize and Cope With It.* New York: Charles Scribner's Sons, 1972.

Mallory, James D. *The Kink and I.* Wheaton, Ill.: Victor Books, 1965.

Maltz, Maxwell. *Psycho-Cybernetics.* New York: Simon & Schuster, 1967.

McDonald, Robert L. *Memory Healing: God Renewing the Mind.* Atlanta: Cross Roads Books, 1980.

McLemore, Clinton W. *Clergyman's Psychological Handbook.* Grand Rapids: William B. Eerdmans Publishing Co., 1974.

McMillen, S.I. *None of These Diseases.* Westwood, N.J.: Fleming H. Revell, Spire Books, 1973.

Menninger, Karl. *Whatever Became of Sin?* New York: Hawthorn Books, 1973.

Minirth, Frank B. *Christian Psychiatry.* Old Tappan, N.J.: Fleming H. Revell Company, 1977.

Minirth, Frank B., and Meier, Paul D. *Happiness Is a Choice.* Grand Rapids: Baker Book House, 1978.

Morris, Desmond; Collett, Peter; Marsh, Peter; and O'Shaughnessy, Marie. *Gestures: Their Origins and Distribution.* New York: Stein & Day, 1979.

Morris, Paul D. *Love Therapy*. Wheaton, Ill.: Tyndale House Publishers, 1974.

Narramore, Clyde M. *Encyclopedia of Psychological Problems*. Grand Rapids: Zondervan Publishing House, 1966.

Narramore, Bruce, and Counts, Bill. *Guilt and Freedom*. Irvine, Calif.: Harvest House Publishers, 1974.

New American Standard Bible. La Habra, Calif.: Lockman Foundation, 1972.

Nierenberg, Gerard I., and Calero, Henry H. *How to Read a Person Like a Book*. New York: Simon & Schuster, Pocket Books, 1971.

_____. *Meta-Talk*. New York: Cornerstone Library, 1978.

Nirenberg, Jesse S. *Getting Through to People*. Englewood Cliffs, N.J.: Prentice-Hall, 1963.

Osborne, Cecil G. *Understanding Your Past: The Key to Your Future*. Waco: Word Books, 1980.

Polston, Don. *There Can Be a New You*. Irvine, Calif.: Harvest House Publishers. 1978.

Poure, Ken, and Phillips, Bob. *Praise Is a Three-Lettered Word*. Glendale, Calif.: Regal Books, 1975.

Rohrer, Norman, and Sutherland, S. Philip. *Facing Anger*. Minneapolis: Augsburg Publishing House, 1981.

Ruesch, Jurgen. *Disturbed Communication*. New York: W.W. Norton & Company, 1972.

Rubin, Theodore I. *The Angry Book*. New York: Macmillan, Collier Books, 1969.

Ruch, Floyd L. *Psychology and Life*. Chicago: Scott, Foresman & Company, 1958.

Shostrom, Everett L., and Montgomery, Dan. *Healing Love*. New York: Bantam Books, 1978.

Skoglund, Elizabeth R. *To Anger, With Love*. New York: Harper & Row, 1977.

Strong, James. *The Exhaustive Concordance of the Bible*. New York: Abingdon Press, 1890.

Swindoll, Charles R. *Improving Your Serve*. Waco: Word Books, 1981.

_____. *Three Steps Forward, Two Steps Back*. Nashville: Thomas Nelson Publishers, 1980.

Torrey, R. A. *The Treasury of Scripture Knowledge.* Old Tappan, N.J.: Fleming H. Revell Company, 1967.

The Zondervan Topical Bible. Grand Rapids: Zondervan Publishing House, 1969.

Thorpe, Louis P.; Katz, Barney; and Lewis, Robert T. *The Psychology of Abnormal Behavior.* New York: The Ronald Press Company, 1961.

Umphrey, Marjorie. *Getting to Know You.* Irvine, Calif.: Harvest House Publishers, 1976.

Vine, W. E. *An Expository Dictionary of New Testament Words.* Old Tappan, N.J.: Fleming H. Revell Company, 1940.

Wagner, Maurice E. *Put It All Together.* Grand Rapids: Zondervan Publishing Company, 1974.

_____. *The Sensation of Being Somebody.* Grand Rapids: Zondervan Publishing Company, 1975.

Walters, Richard P. *Anger: Yours and Mine and What to Do About It.* Grand Rapids: Zondervan Publishing House, 1981.

Wahlroos, Sven. *Family Communication.* New York: New American Library, Signet Books, 1974.

Wright, Norman. *An Answer to Anger and Frustration.* Irvine, Calif.: Harvest House Publishers, 1977.

_____. *Living Beyond Worry and Anger.* Irvine, Calif.: Harvest House Publishers, 1979.

_____. *Marital Counseling: A Biblically-Based, Behavioral, Cognitive Approach.* Denver: Christian Marriage Enrichment, 1981.

_____. *The Christian Use of Emotional Power.* Old Tappan, N.J.: Fleming H. Revell Company, 1974.

_____. *The Pillars of Marriage.* Glendale, Calif.: Regal Books, 1979.

Zimbardo, Philip G., and Radl, Shirley L. *The Shy Child.* New York: McGraw-Hill Book Company, 1981.

Scripture Index

Subject Index